The Notion of Tribe

言不順，則事不成。
各不正、言不順，
子曰，必也正名乎⋯

The Master said, "What is necessary is to rectify names.... If names be not correct, language is not in accordance with the truth of things. If language is not in accordance with the truth of things, affairs cannot be carried on to success."

Confucian Analects, Bk. XIII, Ch. III: 2 and 5. (Translation of James Legge.)

The Notion of Tribe

Morton H. Fried
Columbia University

Cummings Publishing Company
Menlo Park, California · Reading, Massachusetts
London · Amsterdam · Don Mills, Ontario · Sydney

This book is in the
Cummings Modular Program in Anthropology

Copyright ©1975 by Cummings Publishing Company, Inc.
Philippines copyright 1975.

Printed in the United States of America. Published simultaneously
in Canada.

Library of Congress Catalog Card No. 75-5309

ISBN 0-8465-1548-2
ABCDEFGHIJKL—AL—798765

Cummings Publishing Company, Inc.
2727 Sand Hill Road
Menlo Park, California 94025

Preface

The Notion of Tribe assaults the generally held concept of "tribe" by attacking the notion of highly discrete political units in pre-state society. Although we are accustomed to think about the most ancient forms of human society in terms of tribes, firmly defined and bounded units of this sort actually grew out of the manipulation of relatively unstructured populations by more complexly organized societies. The invention of the state, a tight, class-structured political and economic organization, began a process whereby vaguely defined and grossly overlapping populations were provided with the minimal organization required for their manipulation, even though they had little or no internal organization of their own other than that based on conceptions of kinship. The resultant form was that of the tribe.

This book presents comparative ethnological evidence to show that tribes, as conventionally conceived, are not closely bounded populations in either territorial or demographic senses. They are not economically and politically integrated and display political organization under hierarchial leaders only as a result of contact with already existing states, although such contact may be quite indirect. They are not either war or peace groups and rarely if ever show congruence with language communities or with religious communities.

Nothing is more quixotic than to attempt to change the meaning of a word firmly rooted in the lexicon. The intention of this assault is to sensitize the reader to a battery of preconceptions about the nature of pre-state society.

Acknowledgments

Even a little book like this one is the result of myriad
stimulations and supports from all too onymous hordes.
Nevertheless, I owe a special debt to William S. Willis,
Jr., friend, anthropologist, and critic, who once again has
supplied both support and wisdom. William Sturtevant
set me in the direction of Kroeber's work, and Lowell
John Bean helped with specific references. Lillian Lent
surmounted great odds in preparing the manuscript from
often untidy copy. Gene Hammel said some very nice
things and asked some hard questions. Ward Goodenough
and Joseph Casagrande were kind with editorial help.
Milton Hess, James L. Nolan, and Martin Weiss made
bibliographic suggestions. These people are responsible
for some of the good things that may be found here,
but whatever is found lacking is the author's fault.

Contents

About the Author

Morton H. Fried received his B.S. from City College of New York and his Ph.D. from Columbia University, where he is currently Professor of Anthropology. He has done field work in China, Guyana, Taiwan, and various places in the Caribbean. Dr. Fried has served in several professional societies, has been a consultant to the National Science Foundation, the National Institute of Mental Health, and the National Endowment for the Humanities, has been a director of the Social Science Research Council, and is the author of several works, including *The Evolution of Political Society*.

Chapter 1

Do Tribes Exist?

Do tribes exist? Or are they chimeras, imaginary com-
pounds of various and, at times, incongruous parts,
societal illusions fabricated for diverse reasons but,
once created, endowed with such solid reality as to
have profound effect on the lives of millions of people? The question is practical, because it does have
consequences in daily life, and theoretical, because
the notion of tribe has played a vital role in various
social sciences, perhaps most conspicuously in anthropology.

There are many words whose meanings are taken for
granted but cannot withstand close scrutiny without
fragmenting into contradictory packets of significance
or dissolving in vagueness. The word "tribe" is certainly among these, subject particularly to the latter
consequence. For that reason, many anthropologists
have attempted to avoid the word, or deliberately isolate it in inverted commas. Part of the trouble is
that the word "tribe" is rooted in the general lexicon, as well as deeply entrenched in the technical
vocabulary of anthropology and other social sciences.
This is simply one specific instance of a widely
spread malady; it is intensified by the fact that
tribe is hardly more rigorously defined in anthropological applications than in popular usage.

Attempts to reform linguistic modes can be virtu-
ous, but quixotic. I hope the reader will discover
more motive behind this reconsideration of the concept
of tribe than the slim chance of decisively affecting

usage. As the argument proceeds, it may be seen that critical examination of this concept offers a vehicle for the discussion of a variety of problems of both practical and academic significance, ranging from the attempt to understand the evolution of human society to the attempt to deal with contemporary problems of intersocietal and intercultural conflict on a variety of levels, from local communities to national states.

Let me begin, deviously, with a line familiar to generations of school children: "Abou Ben Adhem (may his tribe increase!)." The poem goes on to identify its central character as both tribesman and cosmopolite. There is a nice contradiction: tribesman and cosmopolite; the former usually connoting the most narrow and local focus of knowledge and associations, the latter someone who has worldwide rather than provincial interests and loyalties. Leigh Hunt, the poet who created Abou Ben Adhem, was quite specific about this, portraying Abou as one who placed before everything else his love for all his fellow men. Hunt's use of the word "tribe" was inspired. It starts the poem sonorously and swiftly conjures up a remarkably vivid nineteenth century vision of a desert people. But Hunt skillfully manipulates the ambiguities of "tribe" and the reader realizes that Abou's tribe could be the local people into which he was born, or all of those in the world who place first their love of humanity. (On Hunt's tombstone the epitaph reads, "Write me as one that loves his fellow-men.")

Even as a fictional character, Abou Ben Adhem stretches our credulity because, described as tribal, he displays incongruent values which place him at odds with most understandings of loyalty according to which tribespeople are said to operate. Although familiar, the matter is neatly expressed by Sahlins:

> The several sectors of a tribe are graded by
> sociability. High and positive in the inner
> sphere of close kinship, sociability declines as
> the sector of social relations expands, becoming
> increasingly neutral in distant circles and ulti-
> mately, in the inter-tribal field, altogether
> negative. (Sahlins, 1968, p. 18)

Economic exchanges are qualified on the same basis, as are all relations:

> Political behavior is similarly qualified. Weapons of dispute commonly have a segmentary calculus, nicely graded in deadliness in a progression with sectoral distance. Matters should not go beyond heated words in family arguments, and though fists may fly in village brawls and spears be raised in intervillage feuds, the fatal poisoned arrow is reserved for tribal enemies . . . a contrast between tribal and civilized moral orders is suggested—between relative and situational norms as opposed to universal imperatives. (Sahlins, 1968, p. 19)

As Sahlins and many others have noted, the placing of loyalty to an immediate community of kin and neighbors is not exclusively characteristic of primitive or simple social structures. Though it is true that the word "tribe" and its derivatives, such as "tribal," or "tribalism," are frequently reserved for social orders regarded as simple or primitive, thereby serving at least potentially as pejoratives, there are other words with overlapping connotations capable of projecting the same content. The word "clannish" is formally enrolled in the dictionary in just this sense. We are familiar, of course, with the close association of the concept of clan with the concept of tribe; and at times there has been some confusion as a result of overlapping usage.

Having thus presented the problems of the word tribe and placed before you some preliminary considerations, let me digress to consider briefly the etymology of that worrisome word. The Oxford English Dictionary echoes other sources in deriving "tribe" from the Latin tribus, the earliest known application of which was to a trifold division of the people of Rome, identified as the Ramnes or Latins, the Tities or Sabines, and the Luceres or Etruscans. Although very early Roman history remains obscure and contentious, it has long been known that the conception of three tribes being present at the founding of Rome is an ancient political myth, sometimes attributed to Etruscan domination in the sixth century B.C., when the

names "Ramnes," "Tities," and "Luceres" seem to have
designated three Etruscan patriclans (Pelham and Conway, 1911, p. 616). Despite such knowledge, histo-
rians at various times have sought to distinguish the
three Roman "tribes" on a variety of cultural grounds,
including linguistic. So far as I am concerned, the
point is that even the earliest use of the concept of
tribe reveals the same kinds of ambiguity and confusion that continue to plague the term in its most current usage.

Indeed, retreating to times even more distant
than the founding of Rome, we encounter other words in
the spirit of tribus, all showing similar stigmata.
The Greek word phyle is found to have been applied
during Homeric times to groups of uncertain composition. According to historian Victor Ehrenberg,

> The Greeks themselves came into the land as
> "tribes." To what extent during the immigration
> and settlement large tribes divided or small
> tribes united lies outside our knowledge; the
> result certainly was that the tribe already in
> existence, or fragments that subsequently broke
> off, shaped themselves independently into a large
> number of political units. In this, the differ-
> ences between the main tribes (Dorians, Ionians,
> Aeolians) or any special characteristic of any
> one of them played a very small part. (Ehren-
> berg, 1960, p. 8)

Whatever the "tribal" organization of early pre-
Mycenaean Greece, it was superseded by numerous local
monarchies; no unified encompassing state evolved until considerably later. Ehrenberg believes it unlikely that in the period of Achaean civilization (1500-
1000 B.C.) "the Greeks of that age felt themselves to
be a single people, still less a 'nation'." Following
the collapse of Mycenaean power in Greece, according
to Ehrenberg, there was "a general revival of primitive conditions, with political forms to correspond.
. . . After the internal and external decay of the Mycenaean age and its kingship, the tribal order came
again into its own" (Ehrenberg, 1960, p. 11). But the
post-Homeric Greek "tribe" was a curious structure, a
melange of kin and non-kin elements. The develop-

mental thrust, as pointed out by Morgan and Engels,
included at least two major features: (1) the emergence (e.g., in sixth century Athens) of a common
civil law standing "above the legal customs of the
tribes and gentes," and (2) the emergence of a division of labor "firmly enough established in its social
importance to challenge the old grouping of gentes
and tribes," which also saw a division of the population into socioeconomic classes "regardless of gens,
phratry or tribe." (Cf. Engels, 1972, p. 172.) Even
prior to the erosion of Greek tribes, before the ad-
vancing phenomenon of the emergent state, the situation was a confused one. The phylae ("tribes") were
frequently comprised of phratries which, in turn,
were thought to be assemblages of clans (gens).

> Where a link between phratry and tribe did not
> exist, the tribe was the phyle; for that is
> really the name for the tribe. . . , and it seems
> that independent settlements occasionally coin-
> cided with a phyle . . . The west of Greece seems
> to have known no phylae. (Ehrenberg, 1960,
> p. 14)

Once again let me assert the saliency of this
discussion. The nature of the concept of tribe has
been a confused and ambiguous one from its earliest
period of utterance. Scrutiny of the Greek materials,
for example, shows variations in the significance of
kinship, as opposed to non-kin relationship, in the
composition of "tribal" membership. Similarly, variations exist in the degree and type of political cohe-
sion in such units insofar as they represented populations integrated for the achievement of diverse internal or external goals, management of the community or warfare. Finally, before taking leave of this
brief consideration of the classical Greek case, let
me suggest that whatever the tribal situation may have
been, it has not, to my knowledge, been suggested that
"tribalism" provided a substantial barrier to the
formation of classical Greek states. Nor, despite the
tremendously long history of regionalism in Greek
economy and politics, is the absence of centralized
government as a characteristic of classical Greek
polity usually attributed to tribalism. This point is

important because analyses of third world political developments, particularly those relating to Africa, are often couched in the most pessimistic terms, with tribalism being described as an unavoidable obstacle to political modernization. One writer offers a précis, not a caricature, of such views:

> [I]t is likely that the image of a Dark Continent, inhabited by savage black men, remains a central, albeit often unspoken, assumption behind many of our perceptions of African political life. The news from Africa more often than not confirms our black thoughts. The first headlines, two decades ago, triggered off for newspaper readers in the English-speaking world the fearsome image of Mau Mau. . . . The nightmare of savages disembarking at Idlewild to occupy their seats at the United Nations was confirmed by the Congo. Born prematurely amid turmoil, bereft of all prerequisites for political viability, . . . divided into a multitude of tribes, led by political caricatures, the Congo seemed to exhibit during the first half of the 1960s a degree of savage violence which confirmed Joseph Conrad's acumen in selecting that country as his locale (in <u>Heart</u> <u>of</u> <u>Darkness</u>). (Zolberg, 1973, p. 729)

The author of that passage, incidentally, does not believe that "most of the countries of Black Africa are tribal cockpits" with "terrifying potential for violence." He does believe that,

> Like other concepts of this sort, "tribalism" explains too little or too much. . . . When applied to Africa, the concept "tribalism" hides more than it reveals. (Zolberg, 1973, p. 731)

Others, however, are less cautious in dealing with the notion of tribalism. The journalist Colin Legum, for example, regards the phenomenon as worldwide:

> Tribalism . . . is the manifestation of overriding group loyalties by members of a culturally affiliated society to locally based interests which involve tradition, land, and opportunities for survival and growth. (Legum, 1970, p. 103)

> Tribalism is Africa's natural condition, and is
> likely to remain so for a long time to come . . .
> if the experiences of Europe, Asia, and North
> America are anything to go by. There is no rea-
> son to suppose that the forces which have kept
> Yugoslavia's Croats, Serbs, Macedonians, Bos-
> nians, Slovenes, and Montenegrins active in the
> defence and promotion of their ethnocentric in-
> terests will not apply with equal force to Afri-
> ca. (Legum, 1970, p. 102. Legum expands his
> examples by citing the French/English conflict
> in Canada, the Fleming/Walloon struggle in Bel-
> gium, and Welsh and Scottish nationalism in Great
> Britain.)

Returning to the history of the concept of tribe,
let it be noted that the Latin word tribus replaced
the word phylon in Biblical references to the several
groups which were said to have comprised the ancient
tribes of Israel. The Hebrew tribe (matteh, shebet,
or shevet) is said to have been a confederation of
families (mishpahot), but its character is at least as
uncertain as that of the Greek phyle. Whatever the
nature of ancient Judaic social structure, the word
tribe, in the form tribu, is first known in English
(actually Middle English) from about the middle of the
thirteenth century in precisely the Biblical reference to the tribes of Israel. In this sense, the Oxford English Dictionary (Vol. IX, 1933, p. 339) de-
fines tribe as "A group of persons forming a community
and claiming descent from a common ancestor." By the
beginning of the fifteenth century usage of the term
expanded, overlapping with what we today understand as
"lineage" or "line of descent." Thus it was regularly
applied to descriptions of Irish social groups elsewhere described as "families or communities of persons
having the same surname" (Ibid).

It is difficult to say exactly when "tribe" began
to acquire pejorative shading, since the addition to
the term of an invidious quality did not lead to its
abandonment in nondisparaging usage. Nonetheless, the
word tended more and more frequently to be applied to
"a primary aggregate of people in a primitive or barbarous condition" (Ibid), or "a local division of a
primitive or barbarous people," (The New Century

Dictionary and Cyclopedia, Vol. 10, 1911, p. 6465.)
There is also the casually disparaging usage, as in
the phrase "sheeplike or tribal consciousness" used
by Marx and Engels in The German Ideology (Marx and
Engels, 1959, p. 252). At any rate there are many and
substantial reasons for the aversion often displayed
toward use of the term. Yet some commentators, including a number who themselves have third world backgrounds, use the term deliberately to differentiate
what they see as a warm, folk-oriented, non-European
form of society from the cold state of exploitation
and regimentation they identify with metropolitan culture. Despite the latter forms of usage, "tribe" and
its associated linguistic forms may be understood as
dirty words no matter what the intention of the
speaker.

Before passing from the definitions of tribe
quoted in the last two paragraphs, let me acknowledge
a particular ellipsis in the cited words, an omission
which relates to a very specific feature that is sometimes claimed for tribal society, namely selfcontained
sociopolitical dominion. Thus, the Oxford English
Dictionary speaks of a tribe as an aggregate "under a
headman or chief," while the New Century Dictionary
and Cyclopedia asserts it to be a division "united into a social or political community." The age of the
concept of political integration as a characteristic
of tribal status is not easily dated. Some applications, as in the usage of English explorers of the New
World, go back several centuries. Whenever it may have
begun, it is explicit as a theoretical concept in the
work of various nineteenth century writers. An illuminating illustration may be provided from H. S. Maine
(1888, p. 69): "In some cases the Tribe can hardly be
otherwise described than as the group of men subject
to some one chieftain." (cf. Hodge, 1910, p. 815.)

Despite such assurances, the effort to make tribe
congruent with effectively integrated sociopolitical
units turns out to be quite difficult ethnographi-
cally. Most entities that have been called tribes
have not in fact coincided with boundable political
groups. Most have lacked any comprehensive organization of "tribal" extent, while having organizational
elements of other scale, such as is represented by

domestic groups, kin assemblages, local groups, or mo-
bile bands. Other examples, showing higher level political crystallization, often display an awkward lack
of fit between the political unit and other sorting
unit to which the concept of tribe is usually said to
apply. This matter is reverted to at greater length
below; meanwhile I note merely that a political approach fails to supply a masterkey to this troublesome
concept of tribe.

Indeed I think there is no hope for a simple
solution to the problem of tribe. Samuel Johnson
attempted one a couple of centuries ago when he defined tribe as a "[d]istinct body of the people as
divided by family or fortune or any other characteristic." Johnson had a genius for elegant simplicity.
Consider his definition of "nation," a concept closely
related to the notion of tribe: "People distinguished
from other people." Acknowledging temptation, we re-
flect on the burden of the ethnographic record and the
ethnological task and continue the exercise. Lexicog-
raphers, like lepidopterists, may pin their prey to
the page, but such actions do not affect the evolution
of living forms. Tribe is a word that may be said to
live in multiplex and changing real environments and
its use is under constant adaptive pressure.

In the following sections we will explore the
more recurrent features of social organization that
have been associated with the concept of tribe as well
as some of lesser frequency. We will consider the
congruence between units that have been designated
tribes and other kinds of units such as breeding populations and language groups. We will examine tribes
as groups claiming common descent and as aggregates
defined by neighbors or more remote strangers. We
will consider them as named groups, the names sometimes arising from the group itself, but often from
the slanderous references of others. We must treat,
however briefly, the overlapping of groups called
tribal with economic networks and, as already indicated, we must repeat the analysis in the political
aspect. Beyond these areas, we must also inquire into
the identification of tribal groupings with specific
religious cults, pantheons, or other congruent theo-
logical phenomena. Indeed, although unable to give

the problem exhaustive attention, we will consider the tribe as "cultunit," to use Raoul Naroll's contraction for culture-unit.

Having discussed the tribe as a descriptive phenomenon, we will turn to some questions of a more dynamic nature, beginning with a consideration of the question whether it is useful to discriminate a tribal stage in sociocultural evolution. Departing from widespread and long held opinion generally favoring the discrimination of such a stage, I will marshal a number of arguments against it and suggest some alternatives. Not denying the existence of tribe, however, I will suggest, with some indication of the supporting evidence, that the most massive and familiar phenomena of tribalism occur as a consequence of the impinging on simple cultures of much more complexly organized societies. I regard the tribe mainly as a "secondary" phenomenon. While some of its manifestations go back five millenia or more to the appearance of the earliest states, the major locus of tribal formation has been in the period of European colonialism and imperialism. The process of creation of the tribe resembles that of the caste, the minority, and the ethnic group. In some basic cultural senses it also resembles the process whereby "races" are brought into being.

Although I have omitted a protracted discussion of the relationship between tribe on one side, and caste, race, minority and ethnic groups on the other, this essay does include a brief discussion of the relationship between tribe and nation. Throughout the whole there has been an attempt to refer to both theoretical and practical matters, the intention being to show that the topic has considerable relevance for contemporary life.

Chapter 2

Tribes as Breeding Populations

However the concept of tribe is faring among cultural anthropologists, it seems to be thriving among physical anthropologists. The former give evidence of attempting to avoid the term, and sometimes make their disdain clear. But an apparently growing contingent of physical anthropologists, many of whom, in league with geneticists and specialists in various aspects of human biology, are doing important research into the processes of microevolution in human populations, have made the concept of tribe a central point of their theory and method.

Before going more deeply into the notion of tribe being employed in some of the most recent work of physical anthropologists, it is worth noting that the idea that a tribe is somehow equivalent to an inbreeding population is about as old as the formal discipline of anthropology. Indeed, precisely that assertion provided one of the earliest controversies for our subject. More than a century ago J. F. McLennan (1865) invented the terms "endogamy" and "exogamy." He speculated that the original mating condition among humans was inhibited by female infanticide. Artificial imbalance of the sex ratio led males to seek mates outside their natal social groups thus leading to the institution McLennan called "marriage by capture." McLennan identified early population sorting units as tribes; since males in these groups had to capture wives abroad, he called them "exogamous tribes." During succeeding periods, as McLennan

11

reconstructed the evolution of human society, population grew, permitting more fortunate tribes to be
divided into exogamic sections, so that such a tribe,
considered as a whole, might be endogamic. McLennan
drew quick, hostile response, revealing that at least
part of his theory was shallow and in conflict with
empirical evidence from the burgeoning ethnography of
the time. Leading critics emphasized that the concepts of endogamy and exogamy were relative rather
than absolute. Lewis Henry Morgan disputed McLennan
on these grounds. As summarized by Engels, Morgan's
Ancient Society (1877) "developed in full consciousness" the argument that "[t]here is no antithesis
between endogamy and exogamy; up to the present the
existence of exogamous tribes has not been demonstrated anywhere" (Engles, 1972a, pp. 82-83). Following Morgan's now generally discredited scheme for a
unilineal set of stages in the evolution of types of
marriage and forms of the family, Engels continued the
previously quoted statement with the following words:

> But at the time when group marriage still pre-
> vailed—and in all probability it prevailed
> everywhere at some time—the tribe was subdi-
> vided into a number of groups related by blood
> on the mother's side, gentes, within which it was
> strictly forbidden to marry, so that the men of
> a gens, though they could take their wives from
> within the tribe and generally did so, were com-
> pelled to take them from outside their gens.
> Thus while each gens was strictly exogamous, the
> tribe embracing the gentes was no less endoga-
> mous. . . . (Engels, 1972a, p. 83)

Setting aside Engels' attachment to the concept
of a universal stage of "group marriage," his analysis
is marked by a strong strain of common sense, which is
to say logical assumptions so deeply rooted in the
speaker's own culture that they seem beyond question.
This common sense approach is still dominant in technical efforts to understand the phenomena of endogamy/
exogamy. The common sense position combines two major
constituents, bringing together concern with problems
of incest on one hand, and the semilogical, semiempir-
ical belief that "like marries like" on the other.

The latter canon is probably more impressively encountered as the principle of "positive assortative
mating" (Buettner-Janusch, 1966, p. 395). To see a
contemporary example of this fusion of assumptions we
need go no further afield than to the work of Claude
Lévi-Strauss:

> Considered as a prohibition, the prohibition of
> incest merely affirms, in a field vital to the
> group's survival, the pre-eminence of the social
> over the natural, the collective over the indi-
> vidual, organization over the arbitrary. But
> even at this point in the analysis, the converse
> of this ostensibly negative rule has already ap-
> peared. . . . In point of fact, marriage rules
> do not always merely prohibit a kinship circle,
> but occasionally also fix one within which mar-
> riage must necessarily take place, under pain of
> the same scandal as would result if the prohibi-
> tion itself were violated. There are two cases
> to be distinguished here: on the one hand endog-
> amy, or the obligation to marry within an objec-
> tively defined group; and on the other, prefer-
> ential union, or the obligation to choose as
> spouse an individual who is related to Ego in
> some particular way. It is . . . possible to
> pass from preferential union to endogamy, prop-
> erly so called, without any marked change. . . .
> It is advisable . . . to distinguish between two
> different types of endogamy. One is merely the
> reverse of a rule of exogamy and is explicable
> only in terms of this rule; the other—or true
> endogamy—is not an aspect of exogamy but is
> always found along with the latter, although not
> in the same regard, but simply in connection with
> it. From this point of view, any society is both
> exogamous and endogamous. Thus among the Aus-
> tralian aborigines the clan is exogamous, but
> the tribe is endogamous. . . . True endogamy is
> merely the refusal to recognize the possibility
> of marriage beyond the limits of the human com-
> munity. The definitions of this community are
> many and varied. . . . A very great number of
> primitive tribes simply refer to themselves by
> the term for "men" in their language, showing

> that in their eyes an essential characteristic of
> man disappears outside the limits of the group.
> . . . Generally, "true" endogamy simply repre-
> sents the exclusion of marriage outside the cul-
> ture, which itself is conceived of in all sorts
> of ways, sometimes narrowly, sometimes broadly.
> (Lévi-Strauss, 1969, pp. 45-47)

While Lévi-Strauss's view of the Australian
"tribe" as an endogamous population has apparent support in the classical Australian ethnographies, statements identifying "tribes" with endogamy are soft in
two fairly conspicuous ways: in the use of what are at
best vague definitions of "tribe," and in the absence
of concrete empirical data indicating actual demographic conditions. While more recent work has not
changed too much with regard to the former problem, it
does display improvement regarding the latter. In any
event, the more recent anthropological studies seem to
be much more supportive of the position that "tribes"
are not in any strict sense endogamous bodies. An interesting case is offered by the Ngatatjara of the
Gibson Desert in western Australia, studied by Richard
A. Gould in 1966. Although considerable social distance could be shown in separate nomadic desert dwell-
ers from settled aborigine populations at Warburton
Ranges Mission, and though this social distance corre-
lated with the infrequency of intermarriage of these
two populations, it was already quite clear that mechanisms were being established that would effectively
close the gap and raise the frequency of intermar-
riages. (What is more, there is no clarity about the
frequency of "intertribal" marriage among those aborigines grouped together as desert people.) In brief,
one of the mechanisms that interferes with intermarriage between those already settled at the Mission and
those recently arrived or still coming in is the dis-
crepancy between the six-class marriage system of the
former and the eight-class system of the latter.
(Once again, it must be pointed out that in no case is
a particular marriage class system simply congruent
with a single "tribe," hence these systems cannot operate as tribe-isolating mechanisms.) In response to
the contradiction between the system differences on

the one hand, and the desert people's desire to obtain
certain benefits by increasing intermarriage with the
already settled Mission people on the other, "the
desert people have worked out a series of equivalents
between their eight-subsection system and the six-
section system at Warburton" (Gould, 1969, p. 176).
Gould, drawing on the earlier work of Henry Fry, indicates the possibility that techniques of finding
equivalencies between systems, thereby permitting intermarriage, antedate recent contact (Gould, 1969,
p. 177; Fry, 1934, p. 473).

It is quite easy to make the error of equating
endogamy with inbreeding, but the two phenomena are
quite different. I have no difficulty conceiving of a
perfectly endogamous society with the most marvelous
degree of genetic heterogeneity—not because of the
action of the Hardy-Weinberg Rule, but because of the
frequency of extra-group matings. Such matings may
never be acknowledged, or their fruits may never be
regarded as such. There are many ways in which ideology transmutes biological fact.

Indeed, the physical evidence of interbreeding
sometimes ultimately comes to the fore, taking prece-
dence over a variety of explanations advanced to con-
serve the theory of the tribe as breeding population.
An interesting case in point is provided by genetic
studies in Arnhem Land:

it is clear that there is clinal variation from
Bathurst and Melville Islands off western Arnhem
Land, to Groote Eylandt in the Gulf of Carpente-
ria in the east. While extreme values in the
island populations could be explained in terms of
the founder effect and genetic drift between generations (particularly because of polygyny), it
is more difficult to account for the mainland
tribes on the cline. It could be hypothesized
that there is an environmental gradient, but
. . . no obvious environmental gradient is dis-
cernible. . . . An alternative explanation is
migration, and there has probably been some
intermarriage across the two cultural blocks of
Arnhem Land, but it is difficult to assess this
retrospectively. The relative closeness of the

> Gunwinggu-"Murngin" tribes on genetic distances,
> does, however, favour such an interpretation.
> (White and Parsons, 1973, pp. 11-12)

One reason for the proclivity of biologists and
physical anthropologists to assume that inbreeding is
the most natural tendency of human groups is attachment to the logically prior assumption that human
mating behavior fits within the general parameters of
other animal mating behavior. The key may lie in the
observation of a geneticist:

> Migration studies on many different species have
> shown that mating outside a central home-base de-
> creases in frequency with increasing distance.
> In addition, they have confirmed that the dis-
> tribution of mating frequency over distance tends
> to be leptokurtic. (Swedlund, 1972, p. 327; em-
> phasis in original)

Actually, endorsement of this view and its extension
to human populations undermines the concept of the
tribe as a breeding isolate, since large portions of
any "tribal" population (except for those in extraor-
dinary conditions of physical isolation) find themselves physically closer to people of some adjacent
"tribe" than to fellow members of the aggregate to
which they are said to pertain. In response to this
common occurrence a further assumption is generated—
the notion that each tribe's living space is surrounded by a kind of Hobbesian no-man's land. For the
most part, I consider such notions poorly founded in
the data pertaining to simple societies, but quite
well founded as a projection of fears and hostilities
endemic in stratified and state-organized societies.
This theme will recur later in this book. (See the
sections on "Tribe as War/Peace Unit," "Tribes as
Secondary Phenomena," and "Tribe and Nation."

Returning to the main subject of this section, I
wish to focus on the use made of the concept by those
whose primary interests lie in the field of human
microevolution. Although several research projects
of generally similar intent and design are presently
under way in widely separated regions, perhaps the
most ambitious has been that led by geneticist J. V.
Neel, who pioneered the field. Merely to list the

many publications relevant to this problem that have come from Neel and his associates would consume considerable space. Most deal with gene frequencies and the processes of micro-differentiation among a specific population of Indians living in southeastern Venezuela and adjacent Brazil. Central to the research are two aggregates known respectively as the Yanomama and Makiritare tribes. A major figure in the conduct of the research is Napoleon A. Chagnon, a thoroughly trained cultural anthropologist and gifted enthnographer of remarkable energy and fortitude; presumably it has been Chagnon who has had primary responsibility for guiding the Neel team's thinking about the nature of the social groups whose members are being studied.

Central to the research of Neel, Chagnon, and their associates is the concept of tribe, the importance of which can hardly be overstated, since it helps determine the theoretical orientation of the research as a whole and guides the selection of specific strategies. In general terms, Neel and his associates describe their work as "an effort to characterize in all ways possible the important genetic parameters of a relatively large and undisturbed Indian tribe. . . ." (Gershowitz et al., 1970, p. 515). Use of the term "tribe" is not simply a matter of terminological convenience, a label for the largest aggregates with which they deal. An essential element in their model is relative isolation—social isolation that provides a high degree of breeding isolation. In their formulations, the team members conceive of a tribe as a self-defined and bounded population having actual or potentially agonistic relations along the entire length of its perimeter. What is more, their model assumes a high probability for the killing of women and children in hostile intertribal contacts, rather than adoption or other amalgamation into the community and gene pool of the victors. While not directly relevant to the thrust of this discussion, it is worth noting that the Neel-Chagnon model also incorporates an assumption that socially dominant males will tend to monopolize sexual intercourse, hence perpetuating a phenomenon functionally equivalent to the "founder effect."

The published results of the Neel team's research constantly replicate a particular conclusion: the differences in gene frequencies between villages of a single tribe "are as great as the differences between tribes of American Indians" (Gershowitz et al., 1972, p. 266). This conclusion is remarkably ambiguous in terms of our discussion of the tribe as a relatively isolated breeding population. Equivalent magnitudes of difference between "intratribal" villages and between "tribes" could be the result of random genetic drift, which is what is behind the so-called founder effect.[1] (All notes appear in the back of this book.) On the other hand, if tribes are not really isolated breeding populations, but simply somewhat arbitrary sociocultural aggregations shifting in time and space, then it is likely that there is either continuous or perennial gene exchange through both the vagaries of the marriage system and the much less well-charted sport of extramarital conjugation.

Though I think it fair to say that the members of the team lean on the concept of tribe as an isolating mechanism, they obviously esteem objective observation and reporting, so that one can glean a good many contrary illustrations from their own data and even from some of their general statements. For example, Neel wrote that "as we have observed it, exchange of individuals between villages and tribes, voluntary or forced, is relatively high, especially at the periphery of the tribe" (Neel, 1969, p. 396). A few additional samples may be given from a large literature.   Thus,

> On their northern and western boundaries, the
> Yanomama are in contact with the Makiritare, also
> still a relatively undisturbed tribe . . . it be-
> came apparent that there was genetic exchange oc-
> curring between these two tribes, quite possibly
> along the pattern of much of the genetic exchange
> between the tribal populations of the past. . . .
> (Gershowitz et al., 1970, p. 515)

This easy postulation of past genetic exchange between distinct tribal populations contrasts with the view presented in other writings associated with this group of scientists, tending to imply that intertribal

gene flow is primarily a recent phenomenon. Consider
in this light the following example:

> The two tribes [Yanomama and Makiritare] live
> contiguously, sharing a common border. . . . At a
> number of points the Yanomama, in the process of
> expanding away from their tribal center . . .
> have within the past several generations forced
> the Makiritare out of their old territory. On
> the other hand, recently, with some 20 years of
> peaceful relations between the two tribes, Maki-
> ritare villages have moved deep into Yanomama
> territory, to be near missions. In some areas
> the two groups have now established such amicable
> relations with each other that they live in mixed
> villages. (Chagnon et al., 1970, p. 341)

But reading just a bit further into their work we discover that these investigators

> learned that the Borabuk [a Yanomama village] and
> Huduaduña [Makiritare village] populations lived
> contiguously on the Auaris for some time prior to
> the turn of the century in a mixed village, and
> that some intermarriages took place between them.
> (Chagnon et al., 1970, p. 342)

They go on to admit that, since the history is unknown,

> there is a possibility of earlier intertribal ad-
> mixture in either or both groups [Yanomama and
> Makiritare] previous to ca. 1875, the approximate
> date that the two groups are estimated (by in-
> spection of genealogies and informant's accounts)
> to have lived contiguously. (Chagnon et al.,
> 1970, pp. 342-343)

It is of some consequence to the foregoing that the
known date of the commencement of missionary activity
in this region is 1955. Indeed, the coming of the
missionaries upset relations between the Yanomama and
the Makiritare that had existed for a period of unknown duration. These relations were characterized by
the trade dependence of the Yanomama on the Makiritare, the most desired goods being steel tools and
glass beads. Since the Yanomama had little or nothing

in the way of material goods that they could exchange, groups of them "periodically [took] up temporary residence with the Makiritare: they work for them in order to obtain the necessary and desirable steel tools that make their agricultural economy more efficient" (Chagnon et al., 1970, p. 343). This gives the Makiritare men certain additional advantages:

> One way in which this advantage is expressed is that Makiritare men (in mixed villages) demand and usually obtain sexual access to Yanomama women. . . . During the period of time when the members of Borabuk resided in close proximity to the Huduaduña, men of the Makiritare group persistently had affairs with the Yanomama women, much to the chagrin of the Yanomama men. (Chagnon et al., 1970, p. 343)

These few illustrations hopefully indicate how flimsy is the notion of tribe as a relatively isolated breeding population. One curiosity, however, is that such material seems to have little effect on the continued efforts of the Neel team to deal with tribes as if they really were relatively closed breeding units. In one of Neel's articles in 1972 it seemed momentarily that some of the critical onslaught directed against the notion of tribe had caused him to alter his view, but at the end he simply deepened the relativism of his criteria:

> Thus far we have employed the term "tribe" as if it were a standard categorization. In fact there is continuing debate concerning the precise connotations of the term. Three facts justify our subsequent treatment of the thirty-seven village samples we will describe as having been drawn from a single tribe. (1) As contrasted to their nearest tribal neighbours (Makiritare, Piaroa, Macushi), the Yanomama have a distinctive common culture. . . . (2) Although there are important dialectical differences from one area of the Yanomama distribution to another, even the most differentiated dialects have approximately 70% of the content of a standard word list in common. None of these dialects is closely related to any

of the languages employed by surrounding tribes.
. . . (3) Finally, the various villages appear to
be connected by a web of migration matrices, usually traversed peacefully. Although in the past
there has undoubtably been inter-tribal "migration" to and from tribes such as the Makiritare
and the Maku, this in our opinion was probably
more limited than the inter-village migration and
more often accompanied by a state of overt hostility than intra-tribal migration. . . . Thus,
to the cultural considerations that enter into
the definition of a tribe we add a genetic,
namely a common migration matrix whose boundaries
are only occasionally traversed, and then usually
by virtue of hostile acts. (Neel, 1972, p. 257)

Evidence of a relatively easy flow of marriage
partners from one tribe to another abounds. Rather
than attempt a systematic crosscultural analysis, let
me offer some scattered illustrations, beginning with
data collected in 1909 and analyzed by T. T. Waterman
and A. L. Kroeber. Dealing with 412 recorded Yurok
marriages[2] they found that 56 (some 13.5 percent) were
with a non-Yurok (Wiyot 7, Tolowa 26, Chiluha 3, Hupa
4, and Karok 16). The ethnologists concluded that "on
the whole, language seems to have been a lesser barrier to intermarriage than distance. . . . It is not
contended that language was no barrier, but it evidently was a relatively minor one" (Waterman and Kroeber, 1934, p. 13).
Intermarriage is also attested to on the Northwest Coast:

Time may alter the membership of villages. Men
frequently seek wives in other communities; and
there is considerable intermarriage between Klamath and Modoc and Klamath and Molala to say
nothing of captured women from Shasta, the Achu-
mawi and Atsugewi of the Pit River region,
Paiute, and the tribes beyond the Cascades.
(Stern, 1965, pp. 18-19)

and in Africa, as in these genealogical data referring
to the Hadza, who are called a "small tribe (800 persons)."

> The Hadza have intermarried with their neighbours
> the Isanzu and to a lesser extent with the Sukuma
> and Iramba. . . . For 437 subjects the propor-
> tions of the ancestral components are Hadza
> 79.8%, Isanzu 17.3%, Sukuma 1.7%, and Iramba
> 1.2%. (Barnicot et al., 1972, p. 634)

Intermarriage even occurs in the face of complex
structural problems, such as might be expected to at-
tend, for example, a marriage across a social "boundary" between people practicing patrilineal inheritance
and another practicing matrilineal inheritance. Jack
Goody addresses this problem specifically in a West
African context. He cites the work of David Brokensha
(1966) on Larteh, Ghana, where some 88 percent of marriages were within Larteh "and half the rest from
other Akwapim towns . . . mostly the 'patrilineal'
ones. By close marriage they avoid the matrilineal
threat." Goody continues:

> I raised this problem with Nana Bagyire VI, chief
> of the Guang town of Abiriw. He replied: "If my
> daughter wanted to marry an Ashanti man I would
> try to dissuade her, since the child would be a
> 'lost person', having no inheritance. Indeed my
> niece did marry an Ashanti and when he came to
> see me recently I told him that if he didn't look
> after her well, then the children would be for
> me." (Goody, 1969, p. 127)

The anecdotal case is simply one part of a major process:

> The same situations that exist in Akwapim are
> also found on the western side of northern Ghana
> where there is a distinct boundary between peo-
> ples who inherit movable property matrilineally
> . . . and those who inherit all property patri-
> lineally. The Dagaba and Wiili . . . fall into
> the latter category, the LoDagaba . . . and the
> LoBirifor in the former. . . .
>
> Once again it is not simply juxtaposition that
> occurs; there is also interpenetration as a re-
> sult of the local migrations that have long been
> a feature of the whole area. . . . when initial

> needs had been satisfied, the primary concern of
> the immigrants with regard to their hosts was to
> procure wives, for themselves or for their sons;
> and at the same time, of course, husbands for
> their daughters. To this end they had either to
> adopt a policy of endogamy (unusual in Africa) or
> alternatively to permit marriage to girls from
> the host group. (Goody, 1969, pp. 127-128)

In addition to the random quality of the foregoing illustrative cases, it can be said that they are
clouded because they refer to the time in which the
culture was under serious pressure from metropolitan
societies. In an effort to indicate that the latter
variable might not be of great significance in this
particular case, let us turn briefly to some instances
from New Guinea where contact is very recent and the
practices described are easily traced to precontact
times. Thus, Robert Glasse indicates that the people
of South Fore have grave difficulty attracting mates,
women to be specific, from North Fore. Complications
arise because South Fore is the area par excellence
of kuru, hence "few North Fore or non-Fore are willing
to expose their daughters to the risks of kuru sor-
cery" (Glasse, 1969, p. 27). Is it possible that
otherwise there might be significant movement through
marriage of women into South Fore? Such happens to
be the case in various other New Guinea societies. In
Bena Bena, for example, there are

> no strong marriage preferences and avoidances.
> Moreover, marriages are widely dispersed. Thus
> a sample of sixty wives of Nupa men represent
> twenty-four different tribal groups and thirty-
> five clans. (Langness, 1969, p. 43)

Paula Brown surveyed 656 marriages of men of the
Chimbu-speaking Naregu tribe, finding 289 (44.1 percent) to have been contracted within the tribe. Marriages with other nearby Chimbu tribes amounted to 304
(46.3 percent), including some described as being to
"recent migrants to the region" and others who "speak
a different dialect" (Brown, 1969, p. 91). An additional 44 marriages (6.7 percent) were said to have
been contracted with more remote people, although

these are still Chimbu speakers. Finally, there were 19 marriages (2.9 percent) involving women who were not Chimbu (Brown, 1969, p. 87).

As a final illustration consider the Telefolmin who live on the Sepik River near the border with West Irian. A sample of 136 marriages involving 81 men showed the following distribution: 77 (about 56 percent) were intravillage, and 127 (about 93 percent) were intratribal. Only nine (about 6 percent) were extratribal. However, these data indicate "pre- and post-European marriages" and show that seven of the nine intertribal marriages were pre-European (Craig, 1969, p. 178).

It must be emphasized that the scattered illustrations just given are not intended to prove that all population units that have been called tribes include some outmarriages. I personally believe that careful survey would reveal that most do indeed include some outmarriages, but such a survey has not yet to my knowledge been carried out. I do wish to leave the impression that examples of outmarriages are easy to come by in societies said to be tribal.

Does this mean that the kind of microevolutionary study being pursued by Neel and his associates, and by others elsewhere, must crumble because we would deprive them of the concept of tribe as their basic population unit? I think not. In fact, precisely similar studies happen to be under way which take what I consider to be the most enlightened view of the concept of tribe. Let me then conclude this particular section by citing the relevant words of Gajdusek and Alpers, who are pursuing studies quite similar to those of the Neel-Chagnon team:

> Throughout the highlands of New Guinea, tribal identity has only been established, as in many other parts of Melanesia, as a result of European contact and administration. Before the establishment of Australian administration in the region after World War II, the pattern of village life was so restricted that few individuals knew of the extent of their language group; for the large groups, there were no native people who had visited all parts of the region inhabited by

those speaking their language. Within such a
linguistic group the people were divided into
loose affiliations of "villages". . . . Groups of
villages, at times extending across linguistic
frontiers, were irregularly and loosely affili-
ated into large political units with resulting
marriage ties, property rights, adoption of children, and frequent exchange of members—again,
even across linguistic boundaries. . . . Although
at a given time such confederations were discrete, their geographic pattern was complex.
. . . In fact, separate hamlets of a village
might belong, temporarily, if not permanently,
to different factions. . . . The structure of
these confederations, or social groupings, was
very loose; nowhere in the highlands was there a
true tribal organization, formalized tribal leadership, or hereditary chieftainship. If there is
anything resembling tribal organizations today,
it follows from governmental determination of
linguistic boundaries, appointment of village
leaders . . . , conduct of censuses, and admin-
istration about a European construct of a "named
tribe." (Gajdusek and Alpers, 1972, pp. S7-S8)

It might strike the reader that the emphasis
placed by Neel on the significance of language as a
criterion of tribal differentiation is in some conflict with the opinions expressed in the statements
of Waterman and Kroeber and with the quotation immediately above. Let us take a closer look at language
in this context.

Chapter 3
Tribes as Linguistic Groupings

"Just as each human society has its own culture," remark Ralph Beals and Harry Hoijer (1969, p. 564),
". . . so every society has its own language." There
is striking resemblance between that statement and a
definition of tribe found in the glossary of a widely
adopted anthropology text: "A social group speaking a
distinctive language or dialect and possessing a distinctive culture that marks it off from other tribes."
(Hoebel, 1958, p. 661. Hoebel's definition goes on
and explicitly exempts the notion of tribe from the
necessity of indicating political organization; this
matter is discussed below.) The attempt to equate
linguistic, cultural, and population groupings is not
confined to the synthesizing task of textbooks. Thus,
Robert F. Heizer, compiling a gazetteer of California
Indian languages, territories, and names, states that
"the main tribal units are identified on the basis of
the languages which they spoke. The tribal map is,
therefore, essentially a linguistic map" (Heizer,
1966, p. 8). Taking another tack, Raoul Naroll has
tried with admirable logic and scholarship to replace
the admittedly vague notion of "tribe" (and related
terms) with the more rigorous concept of "cultunit,"
which he seeks to give a substantial linguistic dimension (Naroll, 1964, pp. 287-288). Dell Hymes views
all such approaches as intellectual descendants of
the theories of Johann Gottfried von Herder (1744-
1803), whose critical assumptions in this matter may
be reduced to four:

26

> (1) "One language—one culture"; that is, the ethnographic world can be divided into "ethnolinguistic" units, each associating a language with a culture.
> (2) When the units are demarcated in space (mapped), the demarcation implies a break in mutual intelligibility in virtue of the language, and hence in communication in virtue of the culture.
> (3) The language in question is the medium of communication for the content of interest with regard to the culture in question.
> (4) These boundary relationships (language, culture, communication) have persisted in time. (Hymes, 1968, pp. 25-26)

Although Hymes' analysis is not specifically directed at the concept of tribe, it is generally responsive to questions concerning the relationship between tribes and linguistic groupings; indeed, Hymes offers a general conclusion:

> With regard to the specific question of the tribe, the answer will depend on the ethnologist's decision as to the appropriate definition of "tribe." It is clear now that use of the term "tribe" for peoples hither and yon has no likelihood of finding support in a consistent linguistic correlate. (Hymes, 1968, pp. 43-44)

As Hymes notes, the ethnographic record can readily supply examples "of the failure of linguistic unity and separateness to coincide with cultural units in various parts of the world," going on to cite various aboriginal Australian situations, several in Asia and one in South America (Hymes, 1968, p. 29). Hymes summarizes the point by quoting S. F. Nadel on the African Nuba:

> We . . . meet with groups which, though they are close neighbours and possess an almost identical language and culture, do not regard themselves as one tribe . . . ; and we . . . also meet with tribes which claim this unity regardless of internal cultural differentiation. Cultural and linguistic uniformity, then, does not imply, and cultural and linguistic diversity—at least

within certain limits—not preclude, the recognition of tribal unity. (Nadel, 1947, p. 13)

The fascinating thing about Hymes' critique and
disposal of the theory of congruence of cultural and
linguistic groupings is the way in which he ranges beyond the obvious in his treatment of the theme. He
introduces evidence of consistent multilinguality even
within the domestic residential unit, within the family. He objects to the narrow frame that is provided
when linguistic behavior is identified with speech;
instead he wants us to consider users of language, by
which he means "speakers, hearers, writers, readers,
and all possible combinations" (Hymes, 1968, p. 32).
Illustrating the point insofar as it involves people
who understand more than one language, Hymes' rendition of Sharp's point is "that such communicative
understanding is not associated with any boundedness
of territory, or political, or other social demarcation into fixed units of the 'nation' or 'tribe'
sort." Sharp himself summed up the matter even more
definitely:

> If we cannot delineate societies or communities,
> or discover any structural framework, political
> or otherwise, which might relate to them, we had
> best ignore the ideas of "nations" or "tribes"
> for this area. (Sharp, 1958, p. 3)

Problems of language, particularly of the congruence of linguistic, political, and general cultural units, are not restricted to simple society. We
know that language differences have been and continue
to provide a major source of conflict within modern
nation-states. The United States has various problems
of this kind. Recently, for example, the courts in
some areas have mandated a more liberal use of language other than English to convey voting instructions
and information. There is also the question of dealing with varied linguistic backgrounds in the context
of our system of elementary education. Canada has the
problem of official bilingualism. Sri Lanka has a major problem in the conflicts engendered by the decla-
ration of Singhalese as the official language, with
the consequent displacement of Tamil. Similar prob-

lems exist in India, in Belgium, and other countries.
Historically, China has been plagued by divisions that
often involve linguistically differentiated populations, such as those that distinguish Hakka from Min-
nan, or Cantonese from Tanka. Such divisions do not
supply models applicable to tribal society, but are
much more clearly involved in sociopolitical organization at the level of the state. The consequences of
mutual unintelligibility in or between simple societies are of far less profound significance than in
more complex social organizations, where they massively affect the basis on which individuals enter the
labor force, enjoy differential quanta of social mo-
bility, or gain access to political power.

Ramifications of the problem go beyond the interests of the present paper. Suffice it to say that
for linguists the problem of interintelligibility
poses considerable technical difficulty. The easy
assumptions that are sometimes made about the parallel
splitting of languages and social groups are in opposition to real situations. This is an important
point. Perhaps the most common way that our culture
has of visualizing evolutionary phenomena is in terms
of dendritic diagrams or treelike representations, but
such conceptions can force the data to assume arche-
typal patterns that have little or no relation to actual processes. Once again, Hymes' warning is clear:
he is concerned that assumptions are being made about
the temporal depth of language divergence in situations in which other kinds of cultural boundaries are
being drawn.

> Demarcation of present-day boundaries between
> languages and dialects seems to be relied upon,
> backed up, if at all, by genetic classifications
> at remoter levels. This approach would suffice
> only if it were true that genetic classification
> of languages and dialects mirrors communicative
> history, and if present demarcations of distance
> and closeness had come about by one, irreversible
> process of divergence. Perhaps it is just some
> image that is implicitly in mind. The downward
> branching trees of language families may be un-
> consciously taken as representing the whole of

> linguistic and communicative history.   If so, it
> must be pointed out that genetic relationship is
> generally a poor guide.   (Hymes, 1968, pp. 40-41)

Although Hymes rejects any simplistic pairing off
of "tribes," "nations," or other kinds of "cultunits"
with specifically associated languages, he finds some
attraction in the present writer's conception of the
"emergence of tribes as secondary phenomena, as reaction formations" (Hymes, 1968, p. 44).   He suggests
that in this framework he could find a significant and
relevant linguistic perspective, one that would re-
flect, not "some primitively given demarcation of the
world" but would deal instead with languages "as instruments of human action."

The idea that tribes, whatever else they may be,
are somehow minimal speech communities, turns out to
be no sounder than the notion that they are basic
breeding populations.   Many "tribes" are associated
with languages (in the narrow, non-Hymesian sense)
that are spoken by other "tribesmen" of conspicuously
different cultural orientation.   Other "tribes" sanction simultaneous use of two or more distinct languages, often in variable frequencies, sometimes in
connection with sexual differences.

Given such stereotype-destroying information, we
can only conclude that linguistic mappings are not acceptable as "tribal" mappings.

Chapter 4
Tribes as Named Groups

Compared to the indignities suffered by others, the
Crow Indians, of the territory that is now Montana and
Wyoming and certain adjacent areas of the United
States and Canada, may be said to be fortunate in the
English language rendition of their group name. To be
sure, the Crow usually referred to themselves as
biruke, "us" as opposed to all others. They also referred to themselves as Apsaruke. Robert Lowie (1935,
p. 3) reports that the early French interpreters settled for "corbeaux" or crow as the bird rendered by
that morpheme, although later speakers of the language
told Lowie that Apsaruke was "the name of a bird no
longer to be seen in the country . . . 'a peculiar
kind of forked-tail bird resembling the blue jay or
magpie.'" Of course, these people should be known as
Apsaruke, if they wish, but compared to the naming in-
justices other populations suffer, the Crow have been
blessed, at least in this regard. In fact, most
"tribal" peoples are known to the world at large by
names that have no relation to their own self-appella-
tions. Worse, a good many are called by derogatory
words from the languages of people they consider their
enemies. The common use of pejoratives as so-called
tribal names will be discussed at greater length below. At this point, however, let us briefly consider
some theoretical implications of the use of names to
detect tribal units.
     We may begin with one of the earliest works that
considered the topic of tribe as such. It was written

by an English student of comparative sociology, Gerald Wheeler, who enunciated four criteria of tribe, the first of these being that "the tribal group is . . . marked off by a special name" (Wheeler, 1910, p. 18). Actually, Wheeler claimed no original insight. Among those whose work he drew upon was A. W. Howitt, an ethnographer with considerable experience in Australia, who had written that "tribes-people recognize some common bond which distinguishes them from other tribes, usually a tribal name, which may be their word for 'man' . . ." (Howitt, 1904, p. 41, cited in Wheeler, 1910, p. 16). Considering this matter perhaps more deeply, Wheeler expressed a number of reservations. The difficulty that struck him was that names ran up and down a scale of inclusion/exclusion. The named unit that one ethnographer identified as a tribe was almost sure to include any number of smaller units, each of which had its own discrete appellative. Wheeler wondered at what level the concept of tribe was most appropriately applied. There were additional complications. Some populations were reluctant to divulge certain names, believing them sacred or powerful or dangerous. Wheeler also recognized that some names commonly accepted as tribal designators originated outside the group referred to, sometimes even being unknown to the members of that group.

Despite early sensitivity to this problem, anthropologists continued to rely on conventionally accepted tribal names. Clark Wissler, for example, made "tribes" the critical units in his specific approach to ethnography and also in his more general approach to culture areas. One of his definitions of tribe considered it to be "the group to all of whose members the tribal name will apply" (Wissler, 1923, pp. 48-49). As Aidan Southall has commented (1970, p. 32), Wissler seemed oblivious to the difficulties implicit in his easy usage.

The point is that we have little or no evidence showing that any particular "tribal" name is actually accepted as such by a reasonable portion of those to whom it is applied. Conversely, we are not even certain that some of the names applied from the outside are understood to be accurately inclusive, even among an informed community of outsiders. What we do have

is a welter of cases in which the name that is applied
from the outside is either not used by those to whom
it is applied, or is used with vague or contradictory
meanings.   Take the well-known designation "Yoruba."
As Southall points out, one authority writing half a
century ago advanced the opinion that the name Yoruba
was of foreign provenience (cf. Johnson, 1921, p.
xix).   This is echoed in more recent scholarship:

> The term Yoruba is sometimes said to have been
> derived from a foreign nickname, meaning cunning,
> given to the subjects of the Alafin of Oyo by the
> Fulani and Hausa . . . Yoruba has been commonly
> applied to a large group, united more by language
> than by culture, whose members speak of them-
> selves as Oyo, Egba, Ijebu, Ife, Ilesha, and
> other names of various tribes.   (Forde, 1951,
> p. 1)

Southall's comment on these remarks of Forde is ex-
tremely apt:

> it is debatable whether the latter named entities
> are any more justly designed as tribes than the
> Yoruba as a whole.   (Southall, 1970, p. 37)

If only Southall himself were more guarded in the use
of the term "tribe," I could unreservedly agree with
his summary statement:

> Group names with an ecological referent are com-
> mon all over the world and often show very poor
> correlation with valid divisions between one
> tribe and another on the basis of political, so-
> cial, cultural, and linguistic facts.   (Southall,
> 1970, p. 38)

Another difficulty with tribal names is their
tendency to proliferate, a natural consequence of
their heterogeneous origins and intentions.   Some of
my favorite examples of this phenomenon are found in
the Handbook of South American Indians.   Take, for example, the article by Curt Nimuendajú on the Cawahib,
Parintintin, and their neighbors, in which we find
this passage:

> Names of the Parintintin are: Self-designation,
> Cawahíb, Cawahiwa (kab, káwa, "wasp"); in Mun-
> ducurú, Pari-rign-rign, "fetid Indians"; in Maué,
> Paratín, from the Mundurucú term designating all
> hostile Indians; in Mura of the Autaz River,
> Wáhai; in Mura of the Madeira River, Toepehe,
> Topehĕ (from Mundurucú taypehe=penis?); in Pirahá
> Toypehé; in Torá, Toebehé (from the Mura) or
> Nakazetí, "fierce," in Matanawi, Itoebehe (from
> the Torá) or Tapakará; and in the Lingua Geral of
> the past century, Yawaretá-Tapiiya, "Jaguar Indi-
> ans." (Nimuendajú, 1948, p. 248)

Unlike the self-designation Cawahíb, which seems
to share derivation with the local word for "wasp,"
most self-designating tribal names are said to be one
and the same as the local word for "human being." A
good case is the Eskimo inuit. However, the term by
which we know the Eskimo has no connection with inuit,
but derives from Algonkian, from names applied to the
Eskimo by Cree and Abenaki Indians. The words from
which the name "Eskimo" derives are close in meaning,
denoting "those who eat raw meat."

The use of a morpheme equivalent to "human being"
may be expected to lead to difficulties unless it is
assumed that there is a universal rule whereby
"tribesmen" identify themselves and tribal fellows as
human and all others as not human or not quite human.
I think it will quickly be seen that underlying this
assumption is a Hobbesian view of primitive society
and, what may be worse, a self-serving mechanism that
blunts any effort to establish on-the-ground realities
of social life at the prestate level. In fact, exclusive groups are not characteristic of simple society,
nor is the concept of "human being" narrowly circum-
scribed. The Jivaro offer an interesting case. According to Steward and Metraux (1948, p. 617), there
are many variants of this name: Jibaro, Chiwaro, Si-
waro, Givari, Xivari, Chivari, Givaro, Zibaro, Jivira,
Hibaro, Jivara, etc. The etymology of Jivaro is uncertain; in any case most of those to whom the word is
applied have always preferred šuarä, sometimes rendered "Shuar" or "Shuara" (Harner, 1972, p. 14).
Though Harner remarks that šuarä means "man," "men,"

or people," he tells us that the users of the term
seem to apply it to "any Indian or group of Indians
(as opposed to whites, who are called apačĭ), without
regard to cultural or linguistic affiliation" (Harner,
1972, p. 14). Perhaps the closest thing to a common,
pan-"tribal" appellative is untsuri šuarä (numerous
Indians), although it is difficult to understand how
widely the term is applied. There is some tendency to
use combined terms that specify possibly more limited
populations, such as muraiya šuarä (hill Indians). To
compound the confusion, the earlier account of the Jivaro spoke of them as comprising four main divisions:
the Jivaro proper, the Malcata, the Palta, and the
Bracamoro, with the last group said perhaps to be ex-
tinct. Compare this with Harner's recent remark:

> Today five Jivaroan tribes or dialect groups are
> known to inhabit the tropical forest of Ecuado-
> rian and Peruvian Amazon: the Jívaro; the Achuara
> (Atchuara, Achual); the Huambisa; the Aguaruna;
> and the "Mayna." (Harner, 1972, p. 14)

Only the Aguaruna fail to use the word šuarä in the
general sense, although recent political events will
possibly lead to the world replacement of the word
"Jivaro" by the word "Shuar." Thus, with outside
help, in 1964 there was set up a Federation of Shuar
Centers (Federacion Provincial de Centros Shuaros) to
coordinate political, economic, and social activities.
Harner tells us that

> The Federation also tries to encourage ethnic
> pride through brief daily radio broadcasts trans-
> mitted in Jívaro from its new headquarters build-
> ing in Suçua. To this end, the native term
> "Shuar" (šuarä), has been adopted in preference
> to the formerly locally prevalent "Jíbaro," the
> latter term being felt to connote "savage."
> (Harner, 1972, p. 214)

The abuses third world populations have been made
to suffer range from the horrors of true genocide
through a great variety of lesser wounds, punishments,
and indignities. While there is no comparison between the humiliation of a ridiculous or disparaging
name and the systematic reduction of a population by

economic and political exploitation and discrimination, the former embarrassment can have considerable significance, since it maintains a climate of self-abasement or impotence. The Shuar, who were once known as the Jivaro, are only one of many cases. Another example is found in western Siberia, where there is a people now called Nenetz or Netsi. Formerly these people were known as Samoyed. In some etymologies that designation is derived from Russian roots and is said to mean the "self-eaters," hence "cannibals." (See the Compact Edition of the Oxford English Dictionary, II, p. 2632.)[3]

As I have tried to indicate, the use of pejoratives as group names accomplishes a variety of ends, none more significantly than when the population concerned is in a web of tributary or colonial relations. In such a situation the metropolitan power, with or without conscious intent, may reach out to place the benediction of power on appellatives that in the previous noncolonial or nonimperial situation had only the sanction of sometime usage. Names easily become part of the political means of dividing and conquering, after which, by providing markers and reminders of social distance, they may function to maintain a system of exploitation. Like genealogies and religions, like myths, prayers, and legends, names play shifting but constantly active roles in the chartering ideology of every human society. China provides a wonderful example. The manipulators of the Chinese state through the ages have used names as tools in governance. One of the central concepts in Chinese political thought has been the notion of orthodoxy as a source of strength and stability, with consequent fear and disdain of heterodoxy. One manifestation of the latter is the inevitable tendency of values of all kinds to drift from safe appointed norms. Thus, names are thought to change their denotations by subtle shifts through time and, in parallel fashion, the notes in the ancient Chinese system of music were expected to become gradually corrupted. To prevent the latter, instruments were supposed to be checked against fixed harmonic standards, a jade scale. The related Confucian concept applying to words was cheng ming, the rectification of names, which included, in a

peripheral way, the handling of relations between Han
and non-Han peoples of various kinds.

In its relations with others, the Chinese culture
also dealt with societies at considerably less than
state levels of political integration. The Chinese
vocabulary for some time has included various mor-
phemes that are usually translated into English as
"tribe." An example may be taken from the famous
translation by James Legge of Lun Yu, the Confucian
Analects:

> Chap. XIII. 1. The Master was wishing to go and
> live among the nine wild tribes of the east.
>
> 2. Someone said, "They are rude.
> How can you do such a thing?" The Master said,
> "If a superior man dwelt among them, what rude-
> ness would there be?" (Legge, 1893-1895, p. 221)

Now, the term in this passage that Legge translated
"wild tribe" was I (夷), which was also the name, the
Chinese appellative, for specific "barbarian" people
living to the east, as the words Ti (狄) and Mo (貊)

referred to those living in the north, and Man (蠻)

to those in the south. The combinations I-ti and Man-
ti occur frequently in contexts conventionally rendered by such western usages as "barbarian(s)" or
"tribe(s)," as in The Doctrine of the Mean, where one

finds similar use of Man-mo (蠻 貊) (Legge, 1893-
1895, p. 429; see especially Legge's note 31 on that
page). The Tzu Yuan, a handy Chinese etymological
dictionary, takes up such meanings under entries for
the character chung (種) usually translated as "kind"
or "variety." It notes that the morpheme chung-jen
(種人 "kind of person") was anciently treated in
terms of the I and Ti distinction just referred to,
citing the History of the Latter Han Dynasty as its
source (Tzu Yuan, p. 1110).

Harking back to the characters for I, Ti, and
Man, those with some knowledge of Chinese might have
already noted an additional pejorative aspect of tribal naming. The character representing I is neutral,
but the character Ti includes the element or radical
ch'uan (犬 or 犭), meaning "dog," while Man includes

the radical <u>ch'ung</u> (虫) meaning "insect."   Indeed,
the Chinese used names to indicate sociopolitical distance.   Radicals might be neutral or might show that
those to whom the name applied were human; the latter
was indicated by use of the human being (= "man," 人
or 亻), or they could be equated with beasts or given
the lowest rank of insects.   (For a discussion of this
matter with regard to the ethnology of Southwest
China, see Ruey, 1972.)

Far from being a reliable "natural" guide to the
existence and composition of tribal groups, names
point the way to confusion or worse.   This is not to
question the use of names in the continual political
process of affirmation and assertion of distinct character on the part of diverse population groups and aggregates at various levels of organizational complexity.   The use of ancient names or the coining of new
ones for this purpose is an aspect of the formation of
tribes and ethnic groups as a secondary phenomenon,
usually in conjunction with colonial or imperialistic
pressures.   These, in turn, are most familiarly, but
not exclusively, rooted in the political economy of
capitalism.

Chapter 5

Tribes as Economic Systems

The notion of tribal economy as a specific form of economic integration has long been implicitly subscribed to, but let me begin with the concept as advanced by Malinowski, who used it as a theme in many volumes of his Trobriand ethnography, and spelled it out, although not without ambiguity, in one particular essay (Malinowski, 1921; cf. Malinowski, 1965, Vol. I, pp. 3-48). Perhaps the crux of Malinowski's view lies in his analysis of Trobriand chieftainship in terms of the overriding of strictly local communities. That is to say, Malinowski, whether or not his analyses be sustained (see Uberoi, 1971), saw clearly that an essential element of the concept of tribe was transcendence of the individual community and, pari passu, that tribalism consisted in functions aggregating otherwise discrete villages into an interacting whole. In the Trobriand case, said Malinowski, this was accomplished in various ways, none more important than the institution of chiefly polygyny, with its economic consequences, here summarized by Uberoi:

> Here and there in the Trobriand Islands are found polygamous households of substantial wealth and influence whose head is the "chief" of a group of villages. Such a "district chief," as Malinowski calls him, has taken wives from a number of local lineages, who are therefore his allies, and are obliged to render him gifts and services consisting, mainly, of filling his and his wives' yam

houses each year. A district chief's household
thus integrates, to an extent, the economic activities of a number of village sections, or villages, which also acknowledge the political duty
to stand together in warfare. (Uberoi, 1971,
p. 41)

The other side of the coin is the possibility
that this "tribal" structure actually dissolves in the
shifting of the fortunes of different big-men and
their immediate home bases.[4] As Uberoi notes, C. G.
Seligman, who did ethnographic work in this region before Malinowski, was of the opinion that the larger
areas in which the Trobriand Islands are to be found,
"present no well marked groups which can be called
tribes" (Uberoi, 1971, p. 8). Because of fluidity of
residence, which might see entire hamlet populations
leave one community and move into another 30 or 40
miles distant, because residential/local groups tended
to be so small, and because linkages between hamlets
often spanned considerable distances, Seligman decided
to avoid the use of the term tribe in describing the
social organization of this region (Seligman, 1910,
pp. 8-9). To this datum must be added Malinowski's
own assurances that the hierarchy of "tribal" relations changes as one shifts informants:

Take for instance the unquestionably paramount
chief of Omarakana in his relation to his military rival, the chief of the province of Tila-
taula. . . . A full description of their relationship would be further complicated by the fact
that the military rival would give an entirely
different account from his point of view of the
relationship than would the chief, and that the
opinion of third parties would differ from one
district to another. (Malinowski, 1965, p. 38)

There is no material in the literature, so far as I
know, on which one may base an opinion concerning the
stability through time of any Trobriand "district" described by Malinowski. His picture is substantially
ahistorical. Nor is there any indication that the
ethnographer sought to penetrate this question with
informant help.

I began this digression into Malinowski's anthropology by noting that he was a strong supporter of the concept of a tribal level of economic integration. I think it will be more useful to pick up the argument in more current manifestations, while nonetheless acknowledging the important role that Malinowski played. Let me turn then to a synthesis of elements to be found in the work of various anthropologists and some of the very few economists who address these problems.

The previous discussion of Malinowski's views facilitates our seeing what should be distinctive about a tribal type of economy: it should have mechanisms integrating several otherwise discrete communities into one system of production, distribution, consumption, or some combination of these. Let it be hastily added that for a system to be tribal it is not necessary that its economy constantly work at the tribal level. It is sufficient that it be capable of occasionally functioning at that level. Unless an intermittent capacity for transcending village autonomy is present, the concept of tribal economy dissolves into nebulousness. It becomes indistinguishable from the vague concepts of simple economy or primitive economy. Indeed, it is not unusual to find these terms used interchangeably, as when Manning Nash uses tribal economy to designate the economic aspects of any small-scale, autonomous society, without considering any further kinds or degrees of organization. Thus, Nash is able to remark that "a rural proletariat may replace a tribal society" (Nash, 1964, p. 179), without giving more than a passing glance to the so-called tribal society. For example, Nash notes his belief that in Melanesia "every gardener brings some of the yams from his plot to the chief's house. There the pile of yams grows and grows, and eventually rots, to the greater glory of the tribe" (Nash, 1964, p. 171, emphasis added).

Similar usage is found in the work of the economist George Dalton, who, like Nash and others, has specified various features whereby one may identify the "primitive economy." To begin with, markets may be absent; if present, they do not dominate the organization of production. This point has various corollaries, including a very low level of economic specialization, a general absence of machinery, and very low levels of capital investment. These conditions, in turn, are linked to the fact that noneconomic parameters of social organization, such as kinship, do dominate economic organization and play a substantial role in organizing production. This is another way of stating Karl Polanyi's observation that in such societies the economy is embedded in the general structure of the culture itself. Third, as stated by Dalton (1967, p. 66), "[i]n tribal Africa, products are frequently marketed, but factors almost never." That is, land is usually not alienable from the local or kin group that exercises its usufruct, and labor is not of the wage type. Fourth, as a consequence of the fact that the "tribal producer does not have a payroll to meet" (Dalton, 1967, p. 70), his economic decisions are quite different from those that might be expected according to classical economic theory, with respect to the allocation of factors of production, work style, selection of things to be produced, etc. Fifth, Dalton cites Firth's paraphrase of Marx: Distribution in a primitive economy operates "[f]rom each according to his status obligations in the social system, to each according to his rights in that system" (Firth, 1951, p. 142).

To all of the foregoing I have no great objection since I usually stand with the substantivists in such matters. I must object, however, to the injection of the term "tribe" or "tribal" into the discussion. The critical problem remains that broached by Malinowski: do the operations of the economic processes just enumerated ever function to bind together, in more or less regular and recurrent fashion, a number of otherwise separate villages or communities?

If we seek an answer to this question in the work of Marshall Sahlins, I think we will be frustrated. In his discussion of "Tribal Economics," a chapter in his study Tribesmen (Sahlins, 1968, pp. 74-95), the basic mode of production for the tribal level is styled "'domestic' or 'familial'" (1968, p. 75). According to Sahlins, "the family is to the tribal economy as the manor to the medieval European economy, or the industrial corporation to modern capitalism: each of these is the central production institution of its time" (1968, p. 75). The trouble is twofold: what Sahlins elsewhere refers to as the "DMP" (domestic mode of production) is at least equally characteristic of peasant economy, indeed, his model is acknowledged to have been stimulated to some degree by the work of Chayanov (Sahlins, 1972, pp. 75 ff). Since "peasant" is not infrequently contrasted with "tribal,"[5] this characterization does not seem altogether useful. Furthermore, there is clearly an intermediate term in the equation of manor with medieval European economy, and that term is the feudal state. Similarly, the un- mentioned middle term in Sahlins' third equation is clearly the bourgeois state. Unfortunately, there is no consistent political entity, no political tribe, that can play the intermediate role between Sahlins' terms "family" and "tribal economy."

Once again, it comes down to the simple problem of determining if there is a consistent pattern of organization of otherwise discrete communities into larger aggregates for the achievement of broader pro- ductivity, or patterns of distribution that regularly exceed the local community, or regular patterns of expanded consumption. Let us look very briefly at each of these.

Sahlins sees the domestic mode of production as an institution with an inherent dialectical flaw: the local kin group is beset by centripetal forces that encourage maximization of independence and discrete- ness, but centrifugal forces are active too. Foremost among "the collective finalities" (for Sahlins makes clear that under normal evolutionary conditions it is enlargement of scale and scope that can be expected) is "the primitive headman or chief" who "personifies a public economic principle in opposition to the private ends and petty self concerns of the household economy" (Sahlins, 1972, p. 130). The outcome is the triumph of tribe over isolated domestic units:

> Tribal powers that be and would be powers en-
> croach upon the domestic system to undermine
> its autonomy, curb its anarchy, and unleash its
> productivity. (Sahlins, 1972, p. 130; emphasis
> added)

Sahlins apparently does not see the frustrating possibility that this process can go on, very much as he
indicates, but without any formation of "tribes" as
commonly understood.   Perhaps that is why the two examples that he suggests immediately after the previously quoted statement are Manus and Lele.   The former
relates explicitly to the economic structure of discrete villages, and the Lele example is cited by Sahlins to provide a converse—a system marked by a lack
of authority, which goes a long way to explain its
poverty (Sahlins, 1972, pp. 130-131, citing Douglas,
1963, p. 1).   Sahlins, in turn, attributes this to low
productivity, "underuse of subsistence resources"
(1972, p. 131).   Incidentally, in citing Mary Douglas'
application of the term "poverty" to the Lele, Sahlins
seems to have forgotten his own inspired handling of
the theme:

> The world's most primitive people have few pos-
> sessions, but they are not poor.   Poverty is not
> a certain small amount of goods, nor is it just
> a relation between means and ends; above all it
> is a relation between people.   Poverty is a so-
> cial status.   As such it is the invention of
> civilization . . . (Sahlins, 1972, p. 37; empha-
> sis in original)

If poverty is an invention of civilization, so may be
the commonplace notion of tribe.   Most tribes so
called in the ethnographic literature are the product
of specific political and economic pressures emanating
from already existing state-organized societies.   The
question of whether a small number of tribes took
shape pristinely in the course of the several separate
evolutions of stratification and state organization
that must have occurred in different parts of the
world, I leave for later discussion.   (See the section
on "Tribes as Ideological Groups.")
    The evidence for pristine tribal systems of eco-
nomic production is sparse.   Sahlins is absolutely
correct: at the hypothetical level of the tribal society the overwhelming focus of productivity lies in
domestic units.   Seldom does even a single whole community in all its component domestic units cohere
regularly in production.   Even more rarely does it

happen that two or more communities may combine; more
frequently it will be parts of two or more communities
(and these parts usually have some pre-existing ties,
kin or affinal bonds being the most usual). Rarely,
except in undocumented and impressionistic statements,
is the vision of a tribally integrated episode of production presented. Thus, we are familiar with "tribal
hunts," such as those said to have characterized the
post-horse Plains cultures, when horsemen surrounded
a buffalo herd and killed hundreds of animals (as in
reference to stories, not to actually observed hunts,
in Lowie, 1935, p. 73). While practices varied,
large-scale hunts certainly did take place, and were
known prior to the diffusion of the horse to the
plains. There is ample archeological evidence of buffalo kills, some of which accord with mythical or
other literary accounts mentioning such things as the
piskun, or other types of fall, in which large animals
were driven, sometimes in sizeable numbers, over
precipices. All too frequently such hunting situations are glibly named "tribal" when the labor involved represents individuals drawn from a single
band. An illustration is provided by the Kutenai.
Turney-High (1941, pp. 14, 18-20) states that all the
Kutenai, whom he terms a tribe, are divided into two
gross cultural/linguistic branches, Upper and Lower,
and further into a total of eight named bands, one of
which (the Libby Band) he considers really a "sub-
band" of another (the Jennings Band); yet another (the
Windemere Band), he states, "is quite a modern band
and should not be given separate enumeration."[6] It
also seems that there was general congruence between
band and camp, although bands might fragment and form
smaller camps for ad hoc purposes.

Turney-High's account of Kutenai subsistence activities is challenging for its suggestion that cooperation above the level of band was a recurrent feature of the hunting of certain large animals. Specifically, he was told by informants that the Lower
Kutenai held communal deer hunts, while regarding
bison as quarry for individuals, at the same time
that the Upper Kutenai hunted deer individually, but
organized large-scale bison hunts. Such a hunt pro-
ceeded as follows:

> A vast circle was formed of pairs of scouts about
> a quarter of a mile apart. When one of the pairs
> sighted bison he signalled back to the others.
> . . . There was no attempt to surround a herd.
> . . . A very well mounted man could pick a supe-
> rior animal for the kill. He would then ride
> into the herd and try to separate it from the
> others so that he could kill it easily. The kill
> being made, he selected another and separated it.
> A man on an ordinary mount could not thus pick
> and choose. He had to be content to rush the
> edge of the herd and kill what he could, fat or
> lean.
>
> A man could shoot bison as fast as he could
> draw the bow, but even a good skinner and butcher
> never tried for more than two at a kill. This
> was as much as he could dress in a day, and as
> much as his women could cut up and dry. (Turney-
> High, 1941, pp. 35-36)

Clearly, the bison hunt, even in post-contact times,
with horses, was not quite a "tribal" event. A better
case can be made for the deer hunt as an event drawing
together people of different Kutenai bands. Such a
hunt featured invitations to other Kutenai, but how
regularly and to what effect is not stated. The deer
drive is of additional significance for being communal
in the division of its yield and for being able, during the course of a single lucky day to supply a community's need for a year's supply of venison (Turney-
High, 1941, p. 39).

It seems to me that the "tribal hunt" is mainly
a fiction of ethnographic description. Among the Kutenai, for example, we have no means of gauging the
extent or regularity of participation. Nor have we
any means of distinguishing interband participation
from intertribal participation. We know that the
Kutenai tended to be tremendously hospitable to peaceful strangers, even those originating from populations
with whom they had been in conflict. Piegans, for instance, could join Kutenai bands for as long as they
wished. Given such an understanding of Kutenai society, I argue that the basic mode of production was
primarily domestic, with some band-wide aspects. Beyond that lay an even wider realm of cooperation,

invitation and exchange, but it did not conform to
tribal boundaries.

I have dwelt on the Kutenai because they offer a
concrete illustrative case. It seems to me that
across the broad spectrum of pre-state societies, al-
lowing for ecological variations, the general model
will be the same with regard to this critical point:
there was no tribal mode of production in pre-state
society. This is even more the case with regard to
pre-state agricultural societies. There are no tribe-
wide systems of agricultural labor input. Where labor
aggregates exceed domestic size, it is almost invariably a matter of restricted cooperative exchange, often based upon affinal kin ties, and rarely assembling
individuals from more than a few households in a
single village or a few adjacent villages. Similar
limitations apply to the assembling of labor for ter-
racing or irrigation projects that may occur at this
sociopolitical level.

It is with regard to the distribution of goods
that notions of a tribal level of economic integration
may be quite strong. On one side is the emphasis on
what Marcel Mauss called "tribal feasts" (Mauss, 1966,
p. 277, as rendered in Sahlins, 1972, p. 175); on the
other, what Malinowski referred to in speaking of "the
chief . . . as a tribal banker" (Malinowski, 1937, p.
232). In between is the range of orchestrated reci-
procities that Sahlins qualified as "generalized" and
"balanced." That is, his "tribal" kin-residential
sector includes a small proportion of transactions of
the type he calls "generalized reciprocity" (i.e.,
tending toward altruism and easy sharing without os-
tensible "bookkeeping") and a heavy weight of transactions of the "balanced reciprocity" type (i.e., a less
personal exchange with greater attention to equivalencies and swift quittance); just beyond, in the intertribal realm lies the hostile milieu of "negative
reciprocity," where the Hobbesian dictum (the myth
of the war of all against all) prevails (Sahlins,
1968, pp. 81-86).

Most of the economic exchange that has been
loosely called tribal probably has been domestic. A
much smaller amount may have involved whole communities. It is likely that only a very small amount has

seen the direct participation of networks of communities, even through the use of agents. What may be an example of true tribal structure, albeit on a rather small absolute demographic scale, is presented in Philip Drucker's account of the Nootka. As Drucker (1951, p. 220) makes clear: "The fundamental Nootkan political unit was a local group centering in a family of chiefs . . ." Drucker also calls these social units "lineages" although specifying that the descent that permeated them was of what I would call the "stipulated" type. At any rate, there was a marked seasonal variation in the settlement pattern of these groups; winter saw them in a comparatively large village, but other seasons saw them dispersed, forming much smaller local groups. On this scale it is possible to identify some potlatches as tribal but I do not think I can be contradicted if I say that there never was a Nootka tribal potlatch, since there was never a Nootka tribe in any functioning sense (except as a designation in a totally alien culture, i.e., one or another of the state-organized cultures that at different times asserted suzerainty over the whole area and all its inhabitants). Even on the much smaller scale of de facto participation, the designation "tribal" is tricky, since, as Drucker notes, the actual transactions in potlatch, "in native theory" were confined "to kinsmen invited because of their relationship ties to the giver" (Drucker, 1951, p. 386).

A similar analysis applies to comparable patterns of tribal exchange in the greater New Guinea-Melanesia area. The exemplary work of Rappaport in demonstrating the ecological rationale of long-term periodic feasting, exchange, and warfare among the Tsembaga, "one of about twenty politically autonomous local territorial groups of Maring speaking people" (Rappaport, 1971, p. 60), fits this model to the extent that coordinated activity is geared to clearly local communities.

> There are no chiefs or other political authorities capable of commanding the support of a body of followers among the Maring, and whether or not to assist another group in warfare is a decision resting with each individual male. Allies are

not recruited by appealing for help to other
local groups as such. When a group is in need
of military assistance, each of its members ap-
peals to his cognatic and affinal kinsmen in
other local groups. (Rappaport, 1971, p. 62)

I am acutely aware of the fact that I cannot
prove my theses in a single paper; volumes would be
required to do so. My intention is to present, albeit
programmatically, a set of assertions that contradict
easy assumptions that, in the aggregate, seem to me to
provide anthropology with a perspective that may be
respectably traditional but is nonetheless erroneous.
This is not to say that tribal economies do not exist!
They do, and it is not paradoxical. Tribal economies
can be generated by secondary tribalism. That is, in
response to a variety of very real pressures from existing states, aboriginal societies may be molded into
tribes, one feature of which is the precipitation of a
real tribal level of exchange.

The same may also be true of the generation of a
tribal level of consumption, if the (secondary) tribe
in question is treated by a metropolitan government as
a more or less homogeneous population of wards. A
reservation system is one way of bringing such a condition into existence. Prior to this, or some comparable event, the notion of a tribal level of consumption would seem to be extrapolated from two kinds of
situation. One is the authenticated windfall, whereby
some great consumable becomes available. It is so
huge, and local storage means so limited, that what is
not eaten up on the spot is a total loss. Ethnographic examples of the windfall are diverse, including Great Basin edible seed collections and stranded
whales in Patagonia and along the Northwest Coast.
The other factor that feeds the myth of a tribal level
of economic consumption is the prevalence of what Sahlins calls generalized reciprocity in such societies.
As I have already tried to indicate, however, the
field of such reciprocity is not really congruent with
aggregates usually defined as tribal.

Apart from the conventional trichotomy, production, distribution, and consumption, the economic sector has at least one further major variable which has

played a major role in the concept of tribe. I refer to "ownership," particularly the critical ownership of the strategic resources of a society. For most societies that have been identified as tribal, the single most critical resource to be considered is land.
Thus, one of the anchors of the concept of tribal society is the notion that access to land, whether for gathering, hunting, fishing, or agriculture, is somehow vested in a "tribe." That is to say, preferential domestic usufruct to one side, common membership in a tribe is thought to convey access to basic productive resources.

Unfortunately, discussion of this matter has significant political consequences in the real world we inhabit. Perhaps the most obvious way in which this matter has surfaced is in the litigation between various groups of American Indians and the government of the United States. Cases of this sort have been brought for over a century, but until the Indian Claims Commission Act of 1946 the process was not only stacked against Indian plaintiffs in lopsided judgments,[7] but the very activity of reaching the court was made as difficult as possible. The Indian Claims Commission Act changed the ground rules and thereby improved the Indians' possibilities for success in pursuing their claims. What did not change was the gap in intercultural understanding that usually placed the Indians at a profound disadvantage. Two issues in particular stand out. One of these had a somewhat remarkable resolution. A simplified view of Indian land use showed two sharply conflicting interpretations: in one the Indian pattern was said to integrate intensive land use in restricted areas with limited use in other broader areas; given this interpretation, Indian land use could be averaged out over a fairly large expanse of land, thereby supporting a very extensive claim for compensation. The other interpretation (and I warn again that this is a simplification of actual positions on the matter) was that the Indians, particularly in the California claims cases, made heavy use of a small portion of the lands they claimed at the hearings, and virtually no use at all of the greatest part of those lands. Accordingly, this could have been the basis for drastic cutting of demands, amounting to nearly 80 percent reduction.

What I find remarkable is that the Indian Claims
Commission accepted the former interpretation of land
use, at least in California, placing heavy reliance on
testimony by Kroeber (Stewart, 1961, p. 187). In doing so, the Claims Commission seems at least partially
to have turned its back on the second major point of
controversy, although this action, too, was to the
benefit of the Indian plaintiffs. I refer to the
problem of establishing both title and continuity of
identity of the title holders. Stewart summarizes
thus:

> In accordance with the Indian Claims Commission
> Act and with decisions of earlier claims cases
> that had been reviewed by the U.S. Supreme Court,
> aboriginal Indian title could be established by
> evidence that an identifiable group used and oc-
> cupied a definable area, at the exclusion of
> others, since time immemorial.[8] (Stewart, 1961,
> p. 185)

The concept of "tribe" inheres in this approach; it
was reinforced by the circumstance that suit was
brought by a tribe or aggregate of tribes in each instance. (Julian H. Steward saw the seeming paradox.
The tribes bringing suit were real enough, but were
not necessarily a reflection of precontact social
organization. See Steward, 1970, pp. 114-115. The
phenomenon conforms to what I call "secondary tribalism.") The reason I say that the Claims Commission
did not meet the problem of tribe head-on lies in its
repeated use of the more limited notion of tribelet in
passages such as this:

> It is not necessary that the Indians prove that
> each of the 500 or more tribelets occupied and
> used every acre of the lands they claimed. . . .
> There is comparatively little proof of actual
> occupation and use of specific tribelet areas in
> California . . . however, there is proof by noted
> anthropologists, based upon years of study of
> Indian culture, habitats and ways of providing
> their subsistence, that the Indian groups used
> and occupied the lands in accordance with the
> Indian way of life. [Stewart, 1961, pp. 187-188,

citing Associate Commissioner Louis J. O'Marr in
the Opinion of the Commission, 31 July, 1959 (8
Ind. Cl. Comm. 1, pp. 31-36).]

This is a remarkably enlightened opinion, the product
of an obvious attempt to surmount barriers to intercultural understanding.   It is interesting, then, to
note that not all ethnocentric assumptions were given
up.   O'Marr concluded that despite different conceptions of land use, "higher elevations . . . and some
large desert areas . . . were part of the areas
claimed and defended when necessary by the tribelet
occupying it" (Stewart, 1961, p. 188, emphasis added).
      In fact, there is considerable uncertainty that
such territories were ever defended and even more
doubt that whatever defense might have been mounted
represented the action of a tribe.   According to Julian Steward, "O. C. Stewart's own data . . . show
that neither band nor tribe members did in fact repel
trespassers" (Steward, 1970, p. 136).   Steward's summary opinion of the matter cannot be improved on: "The
concept of tribes among Shoshoneans is an anthropologist's fiction" (1970, p. 147).
      This still leaves the final matter, which was
personally troublesome to Steward because he had been
a witness for the defendant in some of the California
claims cases—and the defendant, of course, was the
United States government.   To argue that such and such
an aggregate of Indians was not a tribe could be tan-
tamount to saying that they were not entitled to some
restitution for the expropriation they and their ancestors had suffered.   It does not much reduce the
moral dilemma of the anthropologist to note that the
question is being put in the classical form of "when
did you stop committing that crime?"   The proper reply
is that the crime was never committed; in the present
case, that tribe is essentially a concept that arises
and thrives in the interactions between state-organized societies and those societies that are not state
organized.   Claims for indemnification should not require post hoc creation of units compatible with the
categories of the state.
      Be that as it may, the anthropologist attempting
to pursue disciplinary interests continually encoun-

ters moral and ethical roadblocks. At the same time
that anthropologists are criticized for demeaning one
people by saying that they were not tribal, they may
be criticized for demeaning another people by saying
that they are tribal.[9] It seems to me that the most
appropriate course is to make quite clear what is involved in the concept of tribe and then apply the les-
sons of this analysis consistently. In this section I
have attempted to give some basis for my assertion
that the concept of tribe as a pre-state phenomenon
has little economic content; that there is no tribal
level of economic activity whether with regard to usufruct or ownership of strategic resources, the organization of productive labor, patterns of exchange, or
consumption.

   One further matter must not be neglected in this
context, since it is a vital part of the history of
the concept of tribe in the last century and has special reference to clashes between modern political
ideologies. Lewis Henry Morgan defined the tribe in
terms of his knowledge of American Indian society, but
he believed that the American Indian "experience,
probably, was but a repetition of that of the tribes
of Asia, Europe and Africa, when they were in corres-
ponding conditions" (Morgan, 1878, p. 112). Morgan
then set down the functions and attributes of such a
tribe, including possession of a territory, a name, a
religious faith and religious personnel, and government, comprising a council of chiefs and perhaps a
paramount chief "in some instances." Ownership of
territory was the first consideration:

> Their territory consisted of the area of their
> actual settlements, and so much of the surround-
> ing region as the tribe ranged over in hunting
> and fishing, and were able to defend against the
> encroachment of other tribes. Without this area
> was a wide margin of neutral grounds, separating
> them from their nearest frontegers if they spoke
> a different language, and claimed by neither; but
> less wide, and less clearly marked when they
> spoke dialects of the same language. The country
> thus imperfectly defined, whether large or small,
> was the domain of the tribe, recognized as such

by other tribes, and defended as such by themselves. (Morgan, 1878, p. 112)

This passage appears in Engels in light paraphrase and
with examples added from German antiquity (Engels,
1972a, p. 153). The view of tribe thus set forth has
become a matter of dogma to Soviet anthropologists,
and to many others elsewhere who consider themselves
Marxists. I think this somewhat ironic, since, in a
sense, it binds them to what is essentially a nineteenth century, bourgeois view of the evolution of
property. It has also inspired numerous academic controversies, some of which, however, have spread to
larger political arenas.

One of the more parochial battlegrounds has been
provided by conflicting interpretations of land ownership among the northeastern Algonkians. Without re-
viewing this widely discussed disagreement at length,
let it suffice here to state the polar positions: on
one side the assertion that Naskapi, Montagnais, Chip-
pewa, and other northern Algonkian-speaking peoples
maintained a system of individual family hunting prop-
erties in a general social milieu described as "atom-
istic"; while on the other it is argued that to the
extent such conditions have been described for these
people they are historically late and the result either of influences from European-derived society or a
reaction to the demands of the fur trade.

What makes this controversy interesting to this
discussion is the contention of at least one Soviet
anthropologist that the forwarding of the notion of
private hunting territories among the northern Algonkian was an attack on the basic conceptions of the
evolution of property so important to socialists. As
put by Julia Averkieva:

> The theory of atomism in primitive societies
> represents the attempt to establish the priority
> of private property and private enterprise, in-
> herent in capitalistic society, in human history
> . . . one more typical example of the transposi-
> tion by bourgeois scientists of capitalistic re-
> lations to remote periods; and by so doing, to
> justify bourgeois avarice in the age of imperial-
> ism. (Averkieva, 1961, p. 212, as translated
> and cited in Hickerson, 1967, p. 318)

The posing of the question, as one between two op-
tions, must be rejected. The alternative to private
ownership of basic resources is not tribal community
ownership, and even the more restricted phrase "communal ownership" may introduce a substantial ethnocentric bias. This is where irony enters. Reading Morgan and Engels one is continually amazed at the
breadth of their vision and the acuity of their analyses, yet both were social products of their times,
permeated with bourgeois notions. These nineteenth
century philosophers could free themselves of a concept of the necessity of individual ownership, or of
family ownership, but in the final analysis they
could not free themselves of the basic notion that
things had to be owned, somehow, by some group. Ownership to them thus meant not merely convenient usufruct, but exclusive possession and the willingness
to resort to violence to protect privileges of access. But in my view of the economics of egalitarian
society (and most ranked societies; see Fried, 1967,
pp. 58-66, 114-133) there are no owners of basic resources, not individuals, not families, not tribes.
That, it seems to me, is what should be meant when
the phrase "primitive communism" is used.
    Denial of the existence of tribes is sometimes
looked on as a reactionary tactic used to deprive
American Indians and some other "third world" peoples
of an inherent capacity for social agglomeration and
leadership, two features indispensable to success in
a world steeped in competition. We are about to look
into the question of the tribe as a political unit.
I can think of no better way to provide a bridge into
that discussion than by quoting a pithy remark of
Hickerson: "equalitarian peoples can cohere without
hierarchies: that is the function of kinship and clan-
ship" (Hickerson, 1967, p. 323).

Chapter 6

The Notion of "Tribelet"

The word "tribelet" has already been encountered in
this paper in the curious context of an official opinion of the U.S. Indian Claims Commission. The context
is surprising, because the term tribelet is restricted
in professional usage and I think rarely encountered
elsewhere. In any event, the word seems to have been
introduced by Alfred L. Kroeber and used mainly by
himself and his students.[10] Kroeber's development of
the term was an outgrowth of his ethnography. Working
with a variety of California Indian cultures in the
early decades of this century, Kroeber became con-
vinced that the simple term "tribe" could not be applied simultaneously to the strongly divergent sociopolitical organizational types represented by the central California Indian societies, those of the south
and adjacent Mexico, and those of the north, going
into Oregon and beyond. Instead, he declared that
there were at least three distinctive forms, with that
prevalent in the central portions being of the variant
he called "tribelet."

Tribes that fit the conventional image tended, in
Kroeber's view, to be those that "lived isolated in
speech and culture among their neighbors . . . therefore had probably solidified into a political coher-
ence well above the usual" (Kroeber, 1955, p. 304).
The examples he gave extended beyond California and
included Kiowa, Comanche, Crow, and Sarcee. Seemingly
true tribes appeared to Kroeber "to have consisted of
not above about 3,000 members," although elsewhere he

says the limit might have been about 5000 (Kroeber,
1955, p. 304; cf. Kroeber, 1948, p. 281). He also referred to such aggregates as "political or state-
tribes," and the California examples were restricted
to the "six or eight nationalities of Yuman stock" including Mohave, Yuma, and Cocopa. Outside California,
he included "the Five Nations of the Iroquois."

By 1932, after several years of increasing doubt
about the efficacy of applying the concept of tribe to
such cultures as the Yuki and the Pomo (a doubt which
infected his predecessor in this ethnography, S. A.
Barrett; cf. Barrett, 1908), Kroeber decided that

> It is thus evident that in much of central Cali-
> fornia there prevailed a type of political or-
> ganization into what may be called "tribelets";
> groups of small size, definitely owning a re-
> stricted territory, nameless except for their
> tract or its best known spot, speaking usually a
> dialect identical with that of several of their
> neighbors, but wholly autonomous. (Kroeber,
> 1932, p. 258)

Kroeber remained satisfied with his coinage of the
term. As he said later,

> I deliberately coined the name tribelet to desig-
> nate it as a sovereign though miniature politi-
> cal unit, which was landowning and maintained
> its frontiers against unauthorized trespass.
> (Kroeber, 1955, p. 307)

The idea of unauthorized trespass, incidentally,
has been explicitly criticized by Julian Steward, who
viewed it essentially as an ethnocentric notion unlikely to be of much use in dealing with societies
such as those Kroeber was considering. As Steward
stated:

> The question is not merely whether an identifi-
> able group or society occupied and maintained
> exclusive use of a delimitable territory. Prop-
> erty in the modern United States . . . implies
> exclusive rights to the land . . . validated by
> a transferable title. . . . Certainly no one
> would argue that the aboriginal Indians attached

> any of these features to their concept of prop-
> erty, despite such common and bare assertions in
> ethnographic monographs. . . . Occasional skir-
> mishes against alien groups can by no means be
> taken as evidence that a society has been mo-
> bilized in defense of territory per se. . . .
> (Steward, 1955b, p. 293)

Steward goes on to make some very interesting statements about the likelihood that the internecine warfare involving Indians was mainly derived from stimuli
provided by the encroachments of European society and
"contingent upon White proximity to or occupation of
their [the Indians'] lands" (Steward, 1956, p. 294).
His view of the derived character of this warfare is
quite like Kroeber's skeptical assessment of the origins of "tribe" among the Indians. Before considering
that assessment, however, let us complete Kroeber's
paradigm by mentioning the third form of pre-state aggregation.

This last form appeared in northwestern California, and was represented by "the Tolowa, Hupa, Chilu-
la, Wiyot, Karok, and, above all, the Yurok" (Kroeber,
1963, p. 105). In brief,

> this area . . . was characterized by extreme
> fractionation. The typical Californian tribelet
> did not occur here. It seems to have been dis-
> solved into separate settlements. The orienta-
> tion of these people was individualistic rather
> than communal. A town or village was a cluster
> of houses and equivalent families, that happened
> to occupy the same site and on the whole got
> along together, but had no basic obligations one
> to the other. (Kroeber, 1963, p. 105)

Whatever the details of organization of such societies, it is evident that they did not fit the conventional mold of tribe which, in Kroeber's definition,
"denotes a group of people that act together, feel
themselves to be a unit, and are sovereign in a defined territory" (Kroeber, 1963, p. 100).

Actually, Kroeber seems to have remained of two
minds concerning the concept of tribe. On one hand,
he continued to use it in a fairly offhand manner

(see, for example, 1948, pp. 299, 302, 400-401, pas-
sim), while on the other he seriously questioned
whether tribes were not the product of European in-
fluence.

> "The tribe" is a minority phenomenon [i.e.,
> present in only a minority of cases]. It might
> yet prove to be wholly a phenomenon of Caucasian
> contact, construal, pressure, or administrative
> convenience. (Kroeber, 1955, p. 312)

> The more we review aboriginal America, the less
> certain does any consistently recurring phenome-
> non become that matches with our usual conven-
> tional concept of tribe; and the more largely
> does this concept appear to be a White man's
> creation of convenience for talking about Indi-
> ans, negotiating with them, administering them—
> and finally impressed upon their own thinking by
> our sheer weight. It cannot yet be fairly af-
> firmed that the current concept of tribe is
> wholly that. But it certainly is that in great
> part, and the time may have come to examine
> whether it is not overwhelmingly such a con-
> struct. (Kroeber, 1955, p. 313)

Kroeber, then, had an early grasp of the phenomenon I
call "secondary tribalism" (see Chapter 12, "Tribes as
Secondary Phenomena"), and this book is submitted precisely because the time could not be more propitious
for a direct confrontation with the concept of tribe.

Chapter 7

The Tribe as a Political Group

In preparing this section I thought it would be wise
to reread some of the materials now regarded as classical in political anthropology. Among these, of
course, is the introduction by Fortes and Evans-
Pritchard to their work African Political Systems. As
I turned the pages I noticed with mounting fascination
that one word seemed to be consistently avoided:
tribe! I was particularly impressed in that section
of their essay that assorted the societies described
in the book between two categories: stateless societies and those with centralized governments. The
word tribe was clearly not needed in this lucid discussion. Alas, on the very last page of the introduction, in what amounts to a trivial usage, certainly
one without serious theoretical implications, the
word appears (Fortes and Evans-Pritchard, 1940, p.
23). A similar tour de force is presented by Paula
Brown in a review of political systems in West Africa,
again demonstrating that a lucid discussion is possible without relying on the word "tribe," although
she, too, succumbs to it at the end, referring to
"tribal ritual sanctions" and "tribal ceremonies"
among the Tallensi (Brown, 1951, p. 276).
      The question, of course, is not whether the word
"tribe" is used in the literature of political anthropology; obviously it is, and very frequently. What
interests me is that nothing is lost in a discussion
that avoids the term; indeed, it is likely to gain
sharpness for the avoidance. Still, it is commonplace

to regard tribes as political units, whether or not
the polity in question is centralized or acephalous,
or possessed of regular positions of authority and
power or not. Conspicuous is the remarkably titled
Tribes Without Rulers (Middleton and Tait, 1958),
which is certainly about social aggregates that lack
clear political center, but not as evidently about
tribes. That is to say, some of the cases presented
in the volume can be described as tribal in structure
only by a cavalier choice of words. The Mandari, a
people of southern Sudan described by Jean Buxton,
offer an interesting case, for in their introduction
to the volume Middleton and Tait scrupulously avoided
applying the term "tribe" to Mandari society. Talking
about "the largest autonomous grouping in political
contexts," they identify this as the "tribe" (their
quotation marks) for the Dinka, Lugbara, Konkomba, and
Nuer, but "the chiefdom" for the Mandari (Middleton
and Tait, 1958, p. 9). They speak of Mandari as
"amalgamations of many different languages and cultures" containing "large groupings of several hundreds
of persons . . . the various groups forming what are
federations each with many chiefs" (1958, p. 15).
Buxton is more direct, saying that "the Mandari are
not a tribe, but a people—a cultural and not a political group" (Buxton, 1958, p. 69). It is important to
note that the main reason Buxton withholds the designation "tribe" from Mandari is that "there is no single Mandari founding ancestor, but certain groups consider they have a more rightful claim to Mandari
country because they occupied their land prior to
people of later advent" (Buxton, 1958, p. 69).

   This has to be compared with Godfrey Lienhardt's
analysis of the Western Dinka, also of the southern
Sudan and also discussed in the Middleton and Tait
volume. Already noted in the previous paragraph are
those editors' acceptance of Dinka tribal status;
Lienhardt actually does not believe that the Western
Dinka, whose population he gives as 234,340 (where the
entire Dinka population is placed by him at 900,000),
comprise a single tribe. Agreeing with the earlier
work of the Seligmans (1932, p. 135), he uses the
phrase: "a congerie of independent and autonomous
tribes" (Lienhardt, 1958, p. 102). He offers a

complicated hierarchy. The Western Dinka, itself
somehow a division of the Dinka ("an ethnic and linguistic group among the Nilotic peoples"), comprises
some six smaller populations (western Luac, Rek,
Abiem, Paliet, Malwal, and Palioupiny), each of which
he calls a "tribal group," and is in turn "an aggregate of tribes," some with as many as 27 different
tribes (Rek), another (Malwal) with only six. Lienhardt asserts that the lands of the tribal groups are
"invariably continuous," but the land of tribes is
not. Furthermore, tribes are divided into subtribes,
which "are the largest fully corporate communities"
(Lienhardt, 1958, p. 103), and large subtribes are
further segmented into sections. The denouement is
quite fantastic:

> When we speak of "the Dinka," we represent the
> people as a totality, known from the outside, so
> to speak, and, to the extent they are all Dinka,
> all equally differentiated from those who are not
> Dinka. No Dinka knows his whole people in this
> way. . . . So, when the Dinka speak of "Dinka"
> jieng, they cannot have in mind all Dinka, as we
> know them to be. . . .
>
> It is only when Dinka from different parts of the
> country meet together among foreigners that their
> common culture and language may draw them togeth-
> er. . . . In their homes, they have no conscious-
> ness of themselves as a nation, and a Bor Dinka
> travelling in Rek country may well find himself
> insulted as a foreigner. . . . On the other hand,
> foreigners who settle with the Dinka . . . are
> accepted as fellowtribesmen. (Lienhardt, 1958,
> pp. 107-108)

Harking back to the point cited in Buxton's work on
the Mandari, concerning the significance of the absence of an ideology of descent from a single common
ancestor, it is interesting to note a somewhat similar, although not completely parallel, situation among
the Dinka. Lienhardt tells us that "the Dinka see the
historical formation of their political groups, not as
the grafting of strangers on to a single original descent group, but as the division of their land between

a number of equivalent original groups which have
spread out and displaced each other on the ground"
(Lienhardt, 1958, p. 128).   In short, what Buxton regards as the minimum characteristic of a tribe is also
lacking in Dinka:

> It is clear that a Dinka tribe has a kind of
> lineage structure. . . . It is equally clear that
> the relationships between all its segments—even
> between the largest, the subtribes—cannot in-
> variably, or even usually, be explained by ref-
> erence to the agnatic genealogy of a single de-
> scent group.   (Lienhardt, 1958, p. 126)

Although the matter cannot be pursued here, the
ethnography of Dinka shows more than passing resemblance to Plains Indian band structure such as displayed by the previously mentioned Kutenai, at least
in terms of the significance of the largest camping
units.   There are many major differences, to be sure,
ranging from the contrast between Dinka unilineality
and Kutenai bilaterality, to the dependence of the
former on domesticated cattle as opposed to the latter's hunting.   But for our purposes, intriguing sim-
ilarities are to be found in the overriding significance of the effective ecological community.   What is
more, the structure of decision and command was equally nebulous in both.   Difficult enough to locate on
the lowest levels of aggregation, it is impossible to
describe any tribal locus of political authority in
either case.

The central difficulty, as I see it, is the confusion that exists between the concepts of chiefdom
and tribe, necessitated by the sort of definition that
offers as a criterion of tribe the organization of a
population which it "unites under one political head,
or chief," as Webster's New International Dictionary
(2nd edition, unabridged), puts it (also see above,
p. 10).   The anthropologist Elman R. Service has taken
pains to distinguish chiefdoms from tribes, making the
latter an evolutionary step out of and beyond the
former.

> A chiefdom occupies a level of social integration
> which transcends tribal society in two important

respects. First, a chiefdom is usually a denser
society than is a tribe . . . second, and more
indicative of the evolutionary stage, the society
is also more complex and more organized, being
particularly distinguished from tribes by the
presence of centers which coordinate economic,
social, and religious activities. (Service,
1971, p. 133)

On the other hand, Marshall D. Sahlins includes tribes
and chiefdom together:

Tribes present a notable range of evolutionary
developments . . . which counterposes at the
extremes two radically different types. At the
underdeveloped end of the spectrum, barely constituting an advance over hunters, stand tribes
socially and politically fragmented and in their
economics undiversified and modestly endowed.
These are segmentary tribes proper. But in its
most developed expression, the chiefdom, tribal
culture anticipates statehood in its complexities. Here are regional political regimes organ-
zied under powerful chiefs. . . . Between the
most advanced chiefdom and the simplest segmentary tribe stand many intermediate arrangements.
We shall concentrate on the widest contrasts: it
will give some idea of the range of development
among tribesmen. (Sahlins, 1968, p. 20-21)

If I were forced to choose between them in this
particular matter, I would have to side with Service.
Sahlins' concept of tribe simply attempts to straddle
too much and collapses; instead of providing a bridge
from simple segmentary organization and acephalous
polities to more complex social aggregates anticipat-
ing the state, Sahlins provides a saltation from the
politically uncoordinated big men of New Guinea and
Melanesia to the highly coordinate paramount chiefs of
Hawaii and Tonga. Sahlins' thesis has the difficulty
of defending the concept of tribe in a political environment as minimal as that provided by, say, Kutenai
or Dinka, and as extensive as Khalka, Kalmuck, or
Fulani (to mix my examples and his). The societies at
the farther end of complexity do not fit most of the

conventional understandings of tribalism, because they display considerable heterogeneity (multiple origins, internal divisions, shifting alignment of component communities, etc.). Those that are at the simpler end of the spectrum, as we have already illustrated elsewhere in this book, are vaguely defined in every dimension as soon as the community level is surpassed. Since this objection applies to Service's concept of tribe as well as the more expansive Sahlins concept, I must actually disagree with both.

In fact, then, there is no "tribal level" of polity. The concept of tribe has been used in connection with totally acephalous organization and with command structures at the veritable level of kingdoms, or at least of emirates. A terminology that implicitly equates one of the old men, who is given to haranguing the young among the Ona, with the khan of the Mongols, cannot be of much use.

Chapter 8

The Tribe as a War/Peace Unit

"Tribal" means nothing concrete with regard to political organization. It does not invariably signify the clustering of a population around a chief or leader. It does not even indicate if the structure of aggregation in the society in question depends on kinship or other kinds of social ties, hence cannot provide any basis for predicting forms of decision-making and allocation. Before we declare the term absolutely devoid of political meaning, however, there is a further functional area that is often brought into the discussion, the realm of organized violence usually called war. One generally political use to which the concept of tribe has been put is vitally tied to war. That is, the tribe is not infrequently portrayed as the utlimate defensive unit of population in pre-state political organization. Conversely, the tribe is sometimes regarded as the largest basic peace field on that level. Let us briefly consider the ethnographic validity of these generalizations.

Citing the work of Henry Sumner Maine, the legal scholar William Seagle discussed the central concept of "the peace of the kindred" which underlies all concepts of sociocultural peace groups from the tiniest community to the most massive state. Even though Seagle showed a prescient suspicion of the notion of "the belligerency of primitive mankind" (Seagle, 1941, p. 44), he seems to echo Hobbes when he says that "in primitive society the peace of the kindred is almost the only peace" (1941, p. 43). The ethnographic fact,

violence and killing are known within both restricted
kin circles and communities in simple societies.
(Their presence in such circles in complex societies
is too well known to need comment. What is attracting
attention in the urban society of the United States is
the frightening growth of murder and violence involving parties who, prior to the assault, have never met
and did not know of each other's existence. Previously, such activity in the urban United States was most
likely to have involved close relatives, affines, or
friends.) There is little question that when such
violence occurs in a simple society, it can produce a
kind of social paralysis; in the absence of retribu-
tive punishments or even rituals it is often met by
inaction. But case material on such violence is rarely comprised of directly observed events; instead, the
record is filled with stories, legends, and myths.

If the local community is widely conceived of as
a peace group, so is the tribe. Kenneth Read, speaking of the Gahuku-Gama of the Central Highlands in New
Guinea, says that "the tribe is the largest group
within which warfare is forbidden, distinguished by a
common name and the exercise of force, and containing
300 to 1000; it is divided into a number of subtribes"
(Berndt, 1962, p. 233, n. 4, discussing Read, 1954,
pp. 34-42). Even within New Guinea, however, there
seems to be rather remarkable variation on this point.
For example, Rappaport (1967, p. 113) says about the
Maring "that fighting between separate territorial
groups is more likely to occur than fighting between
descent groups that are constituents of a single local
population." Settlement of ura amang, Maring for "inside fights," or gui bamp, Maring for "brother
fights," is comparatively quick since there are many
intermediaries whose interests may be endangered by
the conflict (Rappaport, 1967, pp. 110-113). But the
interesting thing is that such fights occur even within the smallest units in the society. What is more,
such fights play a role in the process of fission and
may generate new divisions. Meanwhile, in the Eastern
Highlands of New Guinea, in an area studied by the
Berndts, there seems to be no parallel to the vocabulary items for "inside" or "brother fights" (Berndt,
1962, p. 233, n. 4), but there is an extensive pattern

of fighting between communities that are rather close
in both geographical and social relational terms. Actually, the structural situation is quite similar to
that analyzed by Rappaport and by A. P. Vayda. Enemies tend to be adjacent, sharing larger resource
areas, not separated by natural boundaries such as
rivers or hill crests. They are also extensively in-
termarried.

Ronald Berndt is particularly impressed with the
relation between marital ties and fighting. He re-
calls A. R. Radcliffe-Brown's recital of a Gusii
(Kenya) statement: "Those we marry are those whom we
fight" (Berndt, 1962, p. 411, citing Radcliffe-Brown,
1952, p. 20). Berndt is discussing a population belonging to four major linguistic units: Kamano, Fore,
Usufa, and Jate. Each of these units is made up of a
number of named divisions, or districts, each with its
localized settlements, villages, or hamlets, with a
more or less sedentary population" (Berndt, 1962,
p. 5):

> There is no question of differentiating, as some
> societies do, between the people one fights and
> the people from whom one obtains a spouse. Here,
> in general terms, the two categories coincide be-
> cause both are activities characterizing a close
> social relationship as contrasted with the re-
> lationship existing between strangers. Within
> this interactory sphere are found the bitterest
> and most hostile as well as the most affectionate
> ties. (Berndt, 1962, p. 412)

Neither Berndt nor Rappaport uses the term "tribe";
their monographs, I submit, are rendered more lucid by
the omission, since, instead, they specify much more
precisely what units are involved in instances of violence, cooperation, exchange, or whatever is being
considered. On the other hand, it is clear from their
accounts, as well as from others more prone to speak
of tribes, that small settlements and groups of settlements can be considered peace units only in a relative way and only if more is known about the structure
of agonistic relations in the specific cultural context, which is to say that for many reasons, some cultures are less prone to violence or organized violence
than others of comparable developmental complexity.

Finally, before leaving this topic, let me briefly address two interesting cases in South America, already raised for other reasons. The first of these is
presented by the Yanomama, who are known for their
combativeness and ferocity. While the Yanomama may
have recently been expanding at the expense of such
neighboring "tribes" as the Makaritare, we have already seen that these intertribal relations are not
necessarily hostile, that the Yanomama have a history
of trading with the Makaritare and regard them as superior sources of shamanistic knowledge and power. To
maintain these relations, the Yanomama sometimes assume what can only be called submissive postures.

As a matter of fact, the highest incidence of
Yanomama warfare is within Yanomama. According to
Chagnon (1968, p. 135), the two worst forms of violence in Yanomama are the intercommunity raid and
something called nomohoni ("trick"), whereby one village gets another to feast a third and the guests are
slaughtered (1968, pp. 138-139). In the nomohoni the
intermediate village has fairly close relations with
both the instigators and the victims; actually all may
have such close relations. As for raiding, it is
particularly "common in the center of the Yanomamö
tribe" (1968, p. 135). It takes place between kinsmen, often between villages that not too long before
were a single undivided settlement. The division of
such villages grows out of violence in many cases,
since conflict occurs even within villages, usually as
their populations increase beyond a certain size. In
any event, the notion of "tribe" as peace group often
turns out to be a romantic fiction since the worst
violence may be confined within a population that is
conventionally "tribal."

It is against this background that I would criti-
cize Michael Harner's discussion of Jivaro society.
It will be recalled that Harner considers that something of a no-man's land separates the Jivaro from
their enemies, especially the Achuara (Harner, 1972,
p. 56). But the Jivaro "tribe" is no peace unit.
Harner seeks to distinguish "war," which is "to secure
as many human heads as possible from an alien tribe,
usually the Achuara," from "feud," "the revenge killing of a specific individual in the same tribe"

(Harner, 1972, pp. 182-183). A scrupulous ethnographer, Harner admits that "there is a 'gray' area in which the patterns of feuding and war overlap to a limited degree" (1972, p. 183). It means that in "the absence of tribal political structure" there is "intermittent escalation of intra-tribal feuding" (1972, p. 183). Some light on the frequency of such "escalations" may be shed by Harner's remark, in another context, that "the intensity of feuding within the Jivaro and Achuara tribes makes long-distance travel . . . too dangerous to be undertaken by most men" (1972, p. 120). Also worth noting are patterns of socialization among Jivaro children, described by Harner as isolated

> from peers outside their own polygynous nuclear family, due to extreme dispersion of households in the forest. This isolation is likely to be conducive to a sense of alienation from the rest of the tribe, particularly when coupled with the traditional early morning lectures which fathers give to "make them be careful" in dealing with others beyond the household and which emphasize the deceitful and treacherous characteristics of other tribesmen. (Harner, 1972, p. 88)

Cases could be multiplied, but I think the point is made: tribes as conventionally comprehended social groupings are not necessarily characterized by internal peace. If they are not peace groups, however, they may well constitute war groups. A conspicuous example is furnished, in theory, by the Tiv of Nigeria. In wars between Tiv and non-Tiv, it is supposed to be a case of "all Tiv against the world" (Bohannan, 1958, p. 46). Actually, such a reaction is unlikely, to say the least. Patterns of warfare as engaged in by the Tiv lack the technological means to involve more than small portions of the population of about 800,000 that is sometimes called the Tiv tribe. Even on the smaller scale of actual instances of "inter-tribal" warfare in this region, it seems that there are agreements between potentially opposed segments of different tribes committing them to neutrality, at least for a time. At any rate, it is clear that in reality the tribe does not provide a total reservoir of warriors that might be welded into a unified force.

Before launching into a discussion of the limitations that must inhibit the use of a tribal population
as a source of military power, it is only proper to
note that some cultures described in the literature as
"tribal" are known to history only as pacifists—at
least there is no record or tradition of their fighting, but there are records and traditions saying that
at such and such an encounter with so and so other
"tribe" they ran away. Elman R. Service has an interesting idea about this, arguing that if the hypermili-
tant "tribals" are the product of the impinging, directly or indirectly, of external forces with consequent drastic changes from aboriginal patterns, the
same must also apply to the victims. The upshot for
Service was to consider, although seemingly with
tongue in cheek, tossing out not only the notion of
tribe, but also the band, "in favor of the single
type, the Egalitarian Society" (Service, 1968, p.
167). This type, he believed, would have lacked
both extreme militarism and extreme pacifism, although having some range in the scale and frequency
of warfare and in the complexity of organization for
war.[11]

I do not want to quibble with Service, nor do I
have opportunity here to make a comprehensive case.
Nonetheless, I must at least state a somewhat different position. In brief, I think that some societies
emerged from time to time, and lasted for substantial
generations, in various environments (but probably
ones of relatively less well-endowed natural food resources), in situations of low competition, where com-
bat was sporadic and individual at most, and flight
the most common reaction to the perception of a possibility of violence. But, on the other hand, I do
believe that the massively aggressive small society is
likely to have resulted from a variety of pressures,
most of them ultimately traceable to pressures of expanding state cultures, and largely of demographic
nature.

Once again, I can imagine a reader becoming
restive, irritated by what may seem to be a vision of
the evolutionary process as dependent on skyhook or
bootstraps. Elements of conquest theory are so deeply
imbedded in our notions of the evolution of the state

that it is difficult to imagine the transition from egalitarian to state society without extensive military adventures. Yet, in another setting, I have attempted to show that warfare plays its major role rather late in the evolution of human society. I have argued that technical limitations make it unlikely that models of military organization can provide early stimulation to the growth of the intermediate forms of organization, ranking and stratification, that lead to the state (cf. Fried, 1961; also Fried, 1967, pp. 99-106, 178-182, 213-216).

It should also be pointed out that heavy military organization can readily be associated with the phenomenon of "secondary tribalism"; indeed, it is to be expected in such a developmental setting. I think the greatest examples of that process yet available are those that played so striking a role in the history of much of the Eurasian land mass from about 500 B.C. to the seventeenth century A.D. This was a period spanning the rise of Hsiung-nu power on the northern and western frontiers of the emerging imperial-state of China, and the expansion of Hsiung-nu, Huns, Yueh-chih, and others southward into the Iranian plateau and India, and eastward to Rome. It includes the emergence of the power and domination of the Mongols and the Turks, from Canton to Vienna. Its last gasp seems to have been the great Manchu (Ch'ing) Empire declared in 1644, which expired only in the twentieth century. In these special examples, however, secondary tribalism existed as the prelude to the rise of a massive secondary state. There are probably other examples outside Asia and perhaps less dramatic; the Zulu and the Araucanians come to mind. The secondary tribe, however, is not necessarily the prelude to state formation. It may simply see a protracted period of interaction with and exploitation by a state.

Chapter 9

Tribes as Ideological Groups

If a bunch of people got together and said they were a tribe, wouldn't they be a tribe? The question is not entirely hypothetical. There are quite a few populations now that with all deliberation refer to themselves as tribes, explicitly using the word to designate an inclusive membership group with certain rights and privileges. By what right does some anthropologist come along and try to take this designation away from them? Let us recall that for many of the populations in question, for example, those American Indians who have received settlements from the Indian Claims Commission, the question of constituting a tribe is all-important, since to win their awards they had

> to prove that they had lived upon the lands they claimed from time immemorial, and that they occupied the lands to the exclusion of all other tribes, and that all other tribes recognized their claim and ownership of the land. (Bohanon, 1965, p. iv. Note that this statement, by the chief counsel of the Otoe and Missouria Tribe, adds a further heavy requirement to those already seen in the quotation on page 51.)

There are, of course, different realms of discourse, and what seem to be the same symbols may actually be drastically different things in the different realms. Anthropologists and lawyers tangled at the claims hearings over precisely such problems. The

73

lawyers seemed to have an advantage: their process of
adjudication is hierarchically structured and a Commissioner or a Judge or even a Supreme Court may make
a decision to which others are bound to defer, while
anthropologists cannot achieve more than fragile con-
sensus, even among themselves.

Anyway, anthropologists are aware that the judgments of commissioners, judges, and even of supreme
courts, are culture bound and temporally limited.
They become attenuated through space and time, even
if at their moment of utterance they are thought to
be capable of disposing of power, wealth, and human
relationships.

Apart from truly complex problems of epistemology
roused by the question that began this section, there
are other matters of considerable concern to anthropologists dealing with social aggregates that are pronounced tribes by their membership. Before turning to
these, however, I think it should be said that all
usages of this term, the particular word "tribe," so
far as I know, insofar as they pertain to members of
units so designated, actually arise from or at least
follow after contact with state organized societies.
Consequently, I have little difficulty accepting such
usage. All self-declared tribes are secondary tribes.

In the phenomenon of secondary tribalism, the
designation of the unit tends to be overt and explicit. Nothing, or at least as little as possible, is
left vague. The name or names are stated and alter-
nates may be given; the territory is specified; the
membership is itemized, as are the criteria for membership. I am influenced in making these statements
by knowledge of the sequence of events in American
Indian societies, but the process visible there, although quite obviously taking a somewhat special path
due to the context of United States social and economic institutions, has analogues elsewhere (cf.
Fried, 1952).

The charters of pre-state social groupings including the great variety of types that have been con-
founded under the rubric of tribe tend to be genealogical, ceremonial, mythological, and ineffable. My
point is perhaps conveyed by an illustrative incident.

On May 23, 1959, the Otoe-Missouria Tribal Council in the council house were consulting Bohanon
concerning legal aspects of land matters. Tribal
members were eager to receive payments. . . . The
topic arose as to whether the descendants of Mary
Jane Drips Benoit Barnes should share in the pay-
ment. . . . It seemed that none of the council
had known until recently that before this woman
married Francis M. Barnes, she had taken an allotment on the Nemaha Half-Breed Reservation under the name of Jane Benoist. This fact was
brought to light by the Barnes family in establishing their genealogy.

Kenneth Black, member of the council, in the most
dramatic speech of the day voiced the final challenge.
He said:

["]It was not the custom of my people to keep
written records, and it was never necessary for
one to prove he was an Otoe. All this was a matter of common knowledge, carried by tradition
from one generation to another. Are the Barnes
family Otoes entitled to a share in tribal funds?
Norman Holmes, area enrollment officer, on this
question said that the government would require
proof by written records—not hearsay. From my
youth I always heard from the older tribal members that the Barnes family are white people, and
not Otoes. It is my duty to protect the tribal
funds of my people. On this point I emphatically
say that when Mrs. Barnes, in the name of Jane
Benoist, took an allotment on the Nemaha Half-
Breed Reservation, she thereby severed herself
and all of her descendants from our tribe. That
reservation was established to get the half-
breeds out of the tribe.["]   (Chapman, 1965, pp.
267-268)

In fact, the sentiment voiced by Mr. Black has
failed of universal adoption among Indians most concerned. It has not been possible to keep the "degrees
of blood" separated and accorded proper shares and
privileges. As one member of the tribe has noted:
"The amount of Otoe blood has not decreased; there are

just more people carrying it around" (Chapman, 1965, p. 368). What is truly problematical, however, is not the dilution of genetic heritage, but the erosion of traditional concepts of descent and preferential rules of residence. There is also a rather widespread ideological aspect of the new political tribalism, namely the presentation of tribalism as warm and oriented toward the person, as opposed to the cold, devouring State. Given such an ideological bent, tribal members are likely to stress the openness of tribal structure, as in a conversation between one Mrs. Morris, a Hupa, and Princess Brantner, President, Yurok Tribal Organization, Inc.

> Brantner: "Are you enrolled at the Yurok tribe?"
>
> Morris: "Well, that is what I would like to know, because my mother was born in the Yurok tribe."
>
> Brantner: "Well, I said, did you sign up as a Yurok Indian, or did you sign as a Hoopa?"
>
> Morris: "Well, I am just in the middle. I don't know which one to be."
>
> Brantner: "Well, you will have to decide which one you want to be, because there are many of us that are the same. There is a lot of Indians that belong to the Yuroks, that are half Yuroks or half Hoopas, and they have decided they want to be a Hoopa Indian. . . . So right now we have a chance to eat salmon up here—if you want to eat salmon, you better say you're a Yurok and join us." (State of California, 1955, p. 411)

I am not trying to suggest that this kind of recruiting pitch is characteristic of pre-state aboriginal societies. It seems to me logically and structurally compatible with secondary tribalism, as I have defined it. But I do believe that pre-state social structures were more frequently open than closed, and generally loosely knit rather than tightly woven (so much so, in terms of economic and political organization, as to lack clear-cut boundaries, except in unusual circumstances). That is one of the main reasons, of course, that I object to the usual concept of tribe.

Nonetheless, I recognize that pre-state societies were not totally formless beyond the separate community. Probably the main device for aggregating distinct local groups, communities that is, was not military, not economic, but ideological and ceremonial. The core of aggregation was usually a myth of common descent about which clustered the genealogies, vague and shallow in some societies, sharp and carefully specified in others. Even in the latter cases, however, the genealogies were ultimately what John Gwaltney, following Malinowski, calls "myth charters" (Gwaltney, 1971), which forever suppress and distort genetic facts in favor of political and economic objectives. That this practice is much amplified in the presence of economic stratification, class and caste structures, the bourgeois state, colonialism and imperialism, is certainly true, as Gwaltney points out, although on a smaller scale and perhaps to a more innocent purpose, it can be found in simpler societies as well. It must operate there because, as we have already seen, most of these societies, whether they are called "bands," "tribes," "egalitarian societies," "chiefdoms," or "rank societies" (to give a range of only partially synonymous or nonsynonymous terms), are composite in the short run and all of them are composite in the long run. By composite I mean something close to but not entirely the same as Steward's usage: the inclusion in a single society "of many unrelated nuclear or biological families" (Steward, 1955, p. 143). For me the problem occurs with the word "related." As will be seen, the function of the myth charter is to supply ineffable, emic, ideologically acceptable, proof of relationship. In fact, the people concerned are probably genetically related, although distantly, and perhaps in many alternate ways. They are not all related in the ways prescribed by their society's descent and marriage rules, but this disparity is avoided when it is not negated by ideological means.

Through myths and rituals a population is maintained as a descent group, even when strangers are taken in through migration, warfare, ecological shifting of boundaries, or curious chance circumstances. In the egalitarian societies most usually designated

tribal, I would argue that the most prevalent mode of
reckoning descent is by stipulation. No checking is
done of links in relationship chains, but membership
in a group is the basis for the assumption of all appropriate relationships. (If I am adopted into the
Wolf clan, all male Wolfs of my generation are my
brothers, or whatever the terminology prescribes.
. . . cf. Fried, 1957, p. 23.) Even in ranking societies or beyond, where there are kin groups based on
demonstrated descent (i.e., kin relationships based
on proof of descent, showing the authenticity of all
connecting links), there is still an area in which
stipulation operates. This area may be filled with
groupings such as clans, but in a larger sense it is
in this area that the whole population that shares an
assertion of common identity may lie. This is precisely the area in which myths of "tribal origins"
flourish and rituals are carried out to honor and
maintain crucial aspects of such beliefs.

The literature of ethnography abounds in examples; here is one, from Walapai, that neatly illuminates my argument:

> Once all the tribes of Indians were one, long
> long ago. At this time there were two gods,
> Hama´tavila . . . , the older, and Tu´djupa,
> the younger . . . [Tu´djupa] took a piece of
> . . . reed, and broke it into pieces. The long-
> est strip he called the Mohave, and the next
> longest he called the Walapai; the third he cut
> shorter and called it the Havasupai. . . . With
> the fourth piece he made the Mukwi (Hopi), and
> with the fifth the Paiute . . . , and with the
> sixth the Nyavpe´ (. . . Yavapai) . . . (Mac-
> Gregor, 1935, p. 12)

The members of each different tribe are explicitly
said to be relatives. The god Tu´djupa is quoted to
this effect: "I want you Mohave to know that you are
all related, and to keep peace. You are all one
family, all brothers and sisters. . . ." (MacGregor,
1935, p. 15). As the myth continues, Tu´djupa is com-
pelled for different reasons to send off in different
directions the Mohave, the Paiute, and the Hopi. It
is also revealed that Tu´djupa had created Whites; the

god sends them off to the east, but warns his Walapai children that they have not seen the last of them (1935, p. 26). After these resettlements, Tu´djupa reveals his intention to those still left:

> "This is my plan, to have you [Walapai, Havasupai, and Yavapai] all one tribe, and I have given you directions what to do."

> But the mean people started a quarrel right away, so he separated them and called them Nyavpe´ (Yavapai) . . . [saying] ". . . Once you were Walapai but now you are a different tribe, the Yavapai. Yet you will have the same food and rules as the Walapai." Ever since, the Yavapai have been the enemies of the Walapai. (Mac-Gregor, 1935, p. 25)

Compare the Walapai story with this account of the beliefs of the Chins of Burma:

> All mankind, they [the Chins of Burma] say, is descended from a woman called Hlinyu who laid 101 eggs, from the last laid of which sprang the Chins. Hlinyu loved the youngest best, but he had gone away, and before she found him again the whole world except bleak mountain ranges had been partitioned out among her other children. So the Chin first man got the hills. . . . Unfortunately, Hlinyu appointed the Burman brother to look after him. . . . When the boundaries of the different countries were marked out, the Burman took very good care to mark his with stones and pillars but he persuaded the Chin that tufts of grass were good enough for him. These were all burned away by the jungle fires, and then the despoiled Chin had to live wherever the Burman told him. (Lehman, 1963, p. 32, citing Scott, 1910, pp. 443-444)

There is no question that this kind of origin story, which simultaneously provides for the kinship of all members of the human species and for the existence of sociocultural differences, exploitation, conflict, and warfare, is very widespread. It is important for our particular thesis, however, to note that

it is equally true that such stories lack universal
distribution. In some instances the topic simply is
not broached. In some others, as in a number of
Australian cases, it is handled in somewhat different
fashion. Thus, although as noted by the Berndts
(1964, p. 38), "members of a tribe usually regard one
another as relatives, as contrasted with outsiders.
In other words, their relationships are phrased in
terms of kinship"; the situation is complicated by
the general failure of native Australians to concep-
tualize groupings at this level. This is not at-
tributable to some deficiency in native Australian
intellect; they readily produce a concept of human-
kind and have some remarkably nonlinear notions of
time (which further complicate the analysis of ancestor or origin stories). It is my impression based
on a survey of the ethnographic literature that to the
extent that Australian cultures deal with origin mo-
tifs, they tend to do so within the framework of existing unilineal descent lines and aggregates,
entities that cross conventional tribal divisions and
linguistic groupings (these also being noncongruent)
(cf. Berndt and Berndt, 1964, p. 63).

Similar observations pertain to Australian cere-
monialism. It might be expected on purely logistic
grounds that the bulk of Australian ritual would be
carried out for and by local groups, single camps.
Considering all types of ceremony, this is probably
the case, the unsettling factor being the predomi-
nance in ritual of the very same patrilines mentioned
in the previous paragraph. In the case of the central
Australian Walbiri, for example, Meggitt (1962, pp.
210-212) indicates that the basic unit in the mainte-
nance of "the integration and balance of man, society
and nature" is the patriline, manifested as a group
that Meggitt terms a "lodge." The reason that this is
a source of complication may be found in another remark by Meggitt:

> Although the patriline has a local reference in
> that its lodge is ritually linked with identifi-
> able dreaming-sites, it is not in itself a local,
> residential group; the members do not exclusively
> occupy a defined territory. (Meggitt, 1962, p.
> 212)

But the members of such a lodge enjoy a sufficient degree of localization "to maintain fairly frequent
face-to-face contacts and to act as a corporate group"
(Meggitt, 1962). Conversely, however, it is clear
that particular patrilines are not the exclusive occu-
piers of particular tracts. What is more, sons did
not invariably enter the lodges of their fathers!
(1962, pp. 218-219) Without going further into the
complexities of Australian social organization, I
merely wish to note that although there was a certain
overlapping between local groups and ceremonial
groups, the equation was far from a simple one and
certainly does not justify any correlation of tribe
and ceremonial group. All the more so, since on the
other side, we are assured by the Berndts (1964, p.
41) that "in any case, the largest ceremonial gather-
ings are normally attended by members of more than
one tribe, or more than one language unit. . . ."
At least in Australia, then, ceremonial groups were
usually either smaller than, or bigger than, the
"tribes."

Precisely the same thing may be said about ceremonial organization in the vastly different culture of
the Yakutat Tlingit of southeastern Alaska. Like other Northwest Coast peoples, the Yakutat enjoyed a
variety of ceremonials but those of greatest scale
were undoubtedly the great potlatches. Although such
a potlatch would normally be hosted by the members of
one particular sib (or of a lineage within a particular sib), the guests would comprise persons from at
least one sib from the opposite moiety. In any event,
it is evident that corporate matrilineal kin groups
supplied the basic organizational input. What is
more, it was primarily in theory that sibs were localized. In actuality, many sibs had portions of
their memberships living elsewhere and, what may be
more significant, were accustomed to sharing a village site and its environs with people of other sib
membership. (Indeed, people of other sib membership
might be co-residents in a particular house, and persons of sibs in the opposite moiety might live in the
same village. See de Laguna, 1972, pp. 213, 322.)
Interestingly enough, the English-speaking Tlingit
commonly apply the word "tribe" to the sib (de Laguna,

1972, p. 212), but it was as "sibs" that they concep-
tualized all society; for example, all Americans were
placed in the Eagle moiety (de Laguna, 1972, p. 450),
and related to by this means. This illuminates the
point I made earlier concerning the use of myth and
mythical genealogies. Thus the Tlingit believe that
their sibs

> are not only deeply rooted in the mythical past,
> they are the embodiments today of the very ori-
> gins of the world and of humanity, reflecting
> the natural order and linking men to it by to-
> temic binds. The sibs constitute the eternal and
> unchanging order of the Tlingit people, fixed be-
> cause no individual can exchange or lose his sib
> identity, and because a sib can never, in theory,
> be changed except through the total annihilation
> of all its members. (de Laguna, 1972, p. 211)

In reality, sibs are not so eternal. Warfare may
see survivors enslaved or dispersed. "[R]educed in
numbers, its members have merged with some related
stronger group," states de Laguna (1972, p. 213).
Even more telling, from the point of view of this essay, is the apparent ease of assimilation of non-
Tlingit into Tlingit society, meaning, of course, that
these aliens would either join existing sibs or form
new ones:

> This process of assimilation of foreigners has
> evidently been much more thoroughly carried out
> on immigrant groups from the interior who have
> joined the Tlingit. To judge from the histo-
> rical traditions, there have been many such who
> have become Tlingit sibs. This is undoubtedly
> the case with the [Nexadi] . . . (de Laguna,
> 1972, pp. 450-451)

The ease of moving from an analysis of social
organization to ideology and ritual is a function of
the interpenetration of these aspects of culture. Let
me conclude this section, then, by considering some of
the observations and ideas of Roy Rappaport, who has
made ethnographic study of the Maring of the Central
Highlands of New Guinea the basis of an intense analysis of the role of ritual in the regulation of human

ecological systems.   In brief, Rappaport (1967, p.
229) maintains that ritual is an important element in
achieving articulation of Maring local and regional
subsystems.

> [T]he Tsembaga are participants in an ecosystem
> . . . so are they participants in a regional
> system . . .

> Of course events in the local system affect
> events in the regional system and vice versa.
> Therefore these two systems are not separate sys-
> tems but subsystems of a larger system . . .
> [R]ituals arranged in protracted cycles (up to
> twenty years), articulate the local and regional
> systems. . . . To be more specific, I have inter-
> preted the ritual cycles of the Tsembaga and
> other Maring as regulating mechanisms . . .
> [whose] operation helps to maintain an undegraded
> biotic environment, limits fighting to frequen-
> cies which do not endanger the survival of the
> regional population, adjusts man/land ratios, fa-
> cilitates trade, distributes local surpluses of
> pig. . . . (Rappaport, 1971, p. 60)

Rappaport avoids the use of the word "tribe."   His
Tsembaga, a nucleated population of about 200 people,
he calls a "local population," one of more than 20
local populations that comprise the "regional population" of over 7000 people who speak Maring.   We have
already seen (see p. 67) that violence occurs within
Tsembaga on occasion, and very extensively within
Maring.   There is no tribal structure here in terms
of economic, political, or military relations:

> There are no chiefs or other political authori-
> ties capable of commanding support of a body of
> followers among the Maring, and whether or not to
> assist another group in warfare is a decision
> resting with each individual male.   Allies are
> not recruited by appealing for help to other
> local groups as such.   (Rappaport, 1971, p. 62)

It is precisely the same in the field of ritual:

> The channels through which invitations to dance
> are extended are precisely those through which

> appeals for military support are issued. Dance
> invitations are not extended by one group to an-
> other, but from one kinsman to another. (Rappa-
> port, 1971, p. 62)

As Rappaport puts it in another context: "The atomis-
tic nature of the organization of local populations is
clearly expressed in [this] extension of invitations"
(1967, p. 184).

Even on the simplest cultural levels, social
groups are task-oriented and do not constantly reas-
semble the same standard membership to achieve their
purposes. Different purposes will see the aggregation
of different populations, especially when the tasks
require cooperation beyond the limits of the narrow
residential community—the transient camp or the more
permanent village. Ritual assemblages, religious
congregations, then, may not be expected to be fully
congruent with assemblages geared to other functions.
The tribe is not a consistent, coherent ritual group.

Chapter 10

Tribes as Cultural Units

Since almost all of the foregoing discussion has been concerned with tribes as cultural units of one kind or another, I should begin this section by making clear what it is about. The question has arisen sporadically of whether a tribe represents a kind of natural clustering of culture traits. If you are a purist, you may prefer to think of it as a population distinguished by homogeneity of their own cultural practices, a homogeneity that is enhanced by a manifest contrast offered by all bordering populations of different tribes that carry markedly different cultures. The notion is a simple one and it has been used both implicitly and explicitly as the basis for certain applications of the comparative method in anthropology.

Unfortunately, there is no greater substance to this notion of tribe than any other of which we have already disposed. Indeed, as might be gathered from the preceding discussion, the absence of tight boundaries in breeding, economic relations, political relations, and warfare, is part and parcel of the more general absence of sharp boundaries with respect to the distribution of cultural traits over an area said to be inhabited by a number of tribes. (Proviso: in cases of recent migration, or where special ecological conditions prevail (e.g., a sharp geographical boundary), severe contrasts can be expected, but even these may not correlate with expected "tribal" boundaries. Also, such sharp differences begin an immediate

process of attenuation as cultural elements move more
or less rapidly across the frontier, even in the
presence of continued hostility.)

The culture area conception of Clark Wissler and
earlier ideas of culture circles (<u>kulturkreise</u>) explicitly recognize permeability of local populations
to cultural elements from all over, but mainly from
their neighbors. The emphasis laid by Wissler on the
tribe did not result from his empirical study of the
aggregation of culture traits and complexes at the
minimal associational level, but was a methodological
assumption that preceded his work. His tabulation of
culture elements was in terms of tribal distributions
(Wissler, 1922, p. 217-257). As a matter of fact, the
same assumption is characteristic of all the work in
this field. Tribes are not delineated on the basis of
the overlapping of trait distribution studies; rather,
the trait distribution studies assume the tribe as
their basic counting unit, taking off from there (cf.
Driver and Kroeber, 1932).

I must confess that my major misgiving in attacking the concept of tribe lies in the possible deletion
of this word in the service of the comparison of cultures. The fact that the word tribe in its conventional sense is rendered meaningless by the arguments
of this paper does not mitigate the sense of loss,
curious as that may be. This may be a reaction to
some suggested alternatives. Raoul Naroll's <u>cultunit</u>,
despite its lovely Orwellian quality, encountered a
largely hostile response, although almost all commentators complimented Naroll for undertaking such a
timely task (Naroll, 1964). It is worth noting, however, that Naroll's attempt was at least partially inspired by recognition of the difficulties afflicting
the usage of "tribe" (Naroll, 1964, pp. 283-284). His
suggested substitute, moreover, was intended to be
"useful for comparative purposes, not necessarily for
descriptive ones" (Naroll, 1968, p. 72).

That peoples living adjacent to or near one another, but bearing different tribal names and said to
be comprising different societies, that such peoples
share many cultural traits and at times are much more
alike than different, can be shown in the citation of
a vast number of examples from the ethnographic liter-

ature. But, as Marshall Sahlins (1972, p. 73) remarks, nothing is "scientifically proven by the end-
less multiplication of examples—except that anthropology can be boring."

Chapter ll

The Tribe in Political Evolution

There are many views of the tribe as a stage of organization in the evolution of political society. A widely-read book of the 1920s was titled From Tribe to Empire (Moret and Davy, 1926), and a more recent volume bears the title From Tribe to Nation in Africa (Cohen and Middleton, 1970). Actually, the former book, which was translated by V. Gordon Childe, was originally called Des Clans aux Empires (Moret and Davy, 1923), and its authors were quite definite about the distinction between clans and tribes. Briefly, they argued that unilineal descent groups were the prior form of organization, were in no sense territorial, and ultimately became localized only to the extent that clans lost their proper nature (Moret and Davy, 1923, pp. 13, 15-16, 18). In the final analysis, however, the position of Moret and Davy was that of Eduard Meyer (whom they quote), reserving only one difference, their contention that clans become villages. Otherwise they agree that the population of ancient Egypt was "purely territorial," that "the nomes were the primitive cells" from which sprang the state, and that these nomes "correspond to aggregations of tribes among people who are still on the threshold of civilization" (Moret and Davy, 1926, p. 131; cf. Moret and Davy, 1923, p. 151). Close to Marcel Mauss, Moret and Davy eschewed a conquest theory. They saw a strong but not exclusive role for warfare, especially in increasing the need for a strong chief. However, by far the leading aspect of

the chiefly persona, as they saw it, was generosity;
one was "the chief, the mighty man, who is able to
give plenty of potlatches because he is the master and
dispenser of food" (Moret and Davy, 1926, p. 106; cf.
Moret and Davy, 1923, p. 126).

Very different in detail, but with a similar view
of the priority of the tribe to the state, are the
conquest theorists.   In 1876 Herber Spencer brought
out the first volume of his work Principles of Sociology, in which he developed the idea that societies
evolved from simple to compound to doubly compound.
Warfare was protrayed as an important driving force,
either directly through conquest, or by forcing the
federation to achieve a better method of defense.   In
any case, Spencer stated flatly that: "No tribe becomes a nation by simple growth" (1896, p. 543).   The
line appears in the work of Ludwig Gumpliwicz, who developed the theme of the progress from tribe to state
through conquest (Gumpliwicz, 1899, pp. 116-121).
Franz Oppenheimer, who payed homage to Gumpliwicz,
acknowledging him as his predecessor in conquest theory, made some important additions.   His thesis, bor-
rowed from Marx, was that all states are class societies; that the state is a class hierarchy.   But Oppenheimer believed that most tribal peoples and peasants were sociologically incapable of generating state
organization.   The spark had to come, according to
this theorist, from a very special kind of tribe, such
as those made up of pastoral nomads.   Warlike tribes
of this type, he believed, conquered sedentary, non-
warlike people and instituted the state (Oppenheimer,
1926, pp. 22-81).

Even much later commmentators, who show little
interest in monolithic explanations of state development and who draw on wide resources of ethnography,
old and new, still strike the same basic note, asserting the sequence tribe → state.   A recent example is
offered by Darcy Ribeiro:

> When conceived as a succession of general civi-
> lizational processes, sociocultural evolution has
> a progressive character that corresponds to man's
> rise from a tribal condition to modern national
> macrosocieties. (Ribeiro, 1968, p. 19)

The contrasting approaches to the problem of
stages, or lines of development, in the evolution of
complex political organization are too numerous for
mention, much less critical discussion, here. An interesting recent review has been made by Lawrence
Krader in the context of his own exploration of the
evolution of the state. Krader's conclusion is that
"the state has not one origin but many" (1968, p.
106). Strongly situated among Krader's alternatives,
however, is the tribe → state transition. For example, Krader places ancient Egyptian state formation
among the earliest (without seeing it necessarily as
the earliest) and, following Eduard Meyer and Moret
and Davy, sees the ancient Egyptian state as the result of the fusion of spat, "an independent tribe
(village, cluster, clan)," into large political entities, "districts . . . out of which the larger polities arose, eventually combining into the Egyptian
state" (1968, p. 55). The next sentence is particularly relevant: "In the process of state formation,
tribes defeated and absorbed other tribes. . . ."
I readily admit, however, that for most of his discourse Krader avoids the term tribe (in many contexts
where its use is common), preferring instead to talk
about bands or villages or communities. To some extent, as I have already admitted, it is devilishly
difficult to avoid at least occasional use of a term
so deeply embedded in our ordinary language.
     Currently, the most influential theory of the
rise of the state seems to be the Marxist theory. In
any event, the Marxist position on the evolution of
the state includes the notion of a tribe → state
transition as a key element. As pointed out by Mau-
rice Godelier (1970, p. 147), Marx and Engels elabo-
rated on this position quite some time before en-
countering the work of Lewis Henry Morgan. They did
so in The German Ideology (1844-1845):

     The first form of property is tribal property.
     It corresponds to that rudimentary stage of pro-
     duction in which a people subsists by hunting
     and fishing, from domestication of animals, or
     at most by agriculture. In the last case, it
     presupposes a vast proportion of uncultivated
     lands . . .

The second form of property is communal property
and State property which is encountered in antiquity and which, above all, provides for the
merging of several tribes into a single town
(ville), by contract or conquest, and in which
slavery existed. (Marx and Engels, 1970, pp.
147-148. Author's translation from the French)

The next statement of position expands on this
basic notion and is found in the Grundrisse der
Kritik der Politischen Ökonomie, written in 1857-
1858. The work is not a finished one, but exists more
in the form of notes toward other works; the section
of greatest interest for the present discussion is
that usually referred to in discussion as the Formen,
from the title Formen die der Kapitalistischen Produk-
tion vorhergen. . . , rendered in English as Pre-
Capitalist Economic Formations (Marx, 1964). As is
now well known, it was in this work more than any of
his others that Marx addressed himself to questions of
multiple paths of sociopolitical evolution, considering, albeit briefly and in fragmented fashion, the
problem of the "Asiatic mode of production" as an alternate course. In the same work Marx again stated
his acceptance of an early tribal stage of economic
and political development:

The first prerequisite of this earliest form of
landed property appears as a human community,
such as emerges from spontaneous evolution . . .:
the family, the family expanded into a tribe, or
the tribe created by the inter-marriage of families or combination of tribes. (Marx, 1964, p.
68 cf., Marx, 1973, p. 472, in which translator
M. Nicolaus speaks not of tribe but clan, the
original word in German being Stamm; however,
Nicolaus admits tribe as an alternative translation.)

For Marx the tribe, prior to the appearance of the
state, was the indispensable instrument of ownership
of basic resources:

An isolated individual could no more possess
property in land than he could speak. At most
he could live off it as a source of supply, like

> the animals. The relation to the soil as proper-
> ty always arises through the peaceful or violent
> occupation of the land by the tribe or community
> in some more or less primitive or already histo-
> rically developed form. (Marx, 1964, p. 81)

Actually, Marx conceived of tribes as having two main
forms, dependent on the existence or absence of state
polity:

> The tribes (<u>Stämme</u>) of the ancient states were
> constituted in one of two ways, either by <u>kin-
> ship</u> or by <u>locality</u>. <u>Kinship</u> <u>tribes</u> historical-
> ly precede <u>locality</u> tribes, and are almost every-
> where displaced by them. (Marx, 1964, p. 76)

That distinction led him to conclude that there were,
concomitantly, "different forms of relationship of
communal tribal members to the tribal land" (1964, p.
82) and he attributed these, in a prescient passage,
to differing ecological conditions, although he did
not, of course, use the word. But Marx could not
countenance a propertyless level of human society; not
to define some condition of property was, as already
seen, to treat human beings "like the animals." What
is more, Marx regarded war as a fundamental condition
of primitive life:

> Among nomadic pastoral tribes—and all pastoral
> tribes are originally migratory—the earth, like
> all other conditions of nature, appears in its
> elementary boundlessness. . . . It is grazed,
> etc., consumed by the herds, which provide the
> nomadic peoples with their subsistence. They re-
> gard it as their property, though never fixing
> that property. This is the case with the hunting
> grounds of the wild Indian tribes of America: the
> tribe considers a certain region as its hunting
> territory and maintains it by force against other
> tribes, or seeks to expel other tribes from the
> territory they claim. (Marx, 1964, pp. 88-89
> cf., Marx, 1973:491, where translator M. Nicho-
> laus uses tribe in exactly the same contexts.)

In the final analysis, said Marx, "<u>Property</u> . . .
means <u>belonging</u> <u>to</u> a <u>tribe</u> (community) . . ." (1964,
p. 90). Here, however, Nicholaus translates: "<u>Prop-</u>

erty . . . means belonging to a clan (community)
. . ." (Marx, 1973, p. 492). (In this and previous
cited passages, emphasis occurs in original.) As I
hope I have indicated above (see Chapter 4, "Tribes
as Named Groups"), I believe that the evidence of
ethnography in the total accumulation since the time
of Marx points in another direction. Again, Marx
was prescient in noting that the so-called property
was never fixed, but he could not free himself from
the pervasive bourgeois view that discrimination of
some form of property is what separates humans from
the beasts.

Before concluding this brief survey of the ideas
of Marx and Engels concerning the priority of a tribal
stage in sociopolitical evolution, let us turn again
briefly to L. H. Morgan, for it was his Ancient Society (1877) that provided the basis for Engels' The
Origin of the Family, Private Property and the State
(1884), a connection testified to not only by the
close resemblances between long sections of the books
and by Engels' acknowledgement, but also by the fact
that Marx made extensive extracts from Morgan's work
and also left critical notes to Morgan's work (Engels,
1972, p. 71). According to Morgan:

> The plan of government of the American aborigines
> commenced with the gens and ended with the con-
> federacy. . . . It gave for the organic series:
> first, the gens, a body of consanguinei having a
> common gentile name; second, the phratry, an as-
> semblage of related gentes united in a higher
> association for certain common objects; third,
> the tribe, an assemblage of gentes, usually or-
> ganized in phratries, all the members of which
> spoke the same dialect; and fourth, a confed-
> eracy of tribes . . .

> In like manner the plan of government of the
> Grecian tribes, anterior to civilization, in-
> volved in the same organic series . . .
> (Morgan, 1878, p. 66)

I find it somewhat curious that Morgan, despite
the clear-cut nature of the categories in his "or-
ganic series," is actually equivocal about the origin

of tribes. His simplest living exemplars, which he
took to be the Australian aborigines, are described
throughout Morgan's treatment of them as living in
tribes. (Cf. Morgan, 1878, pp. 50-51, 54-55.) What
is more, in Morgan's thumbnail sketch of the great
"ethnical periods," which comprised the evolution of
culture from the lower status of savagery to civilization, the existence of tribes is implied in the lowest status of savagery in Morgan's oblique comment:
"No exemplification of tribes of mankind in this condition remained to the historical period" (1878, p.
10). Morgan left no doubt in this regard about the
second or middle status of savagery:

> Among tribes still existing it will leave in the
> Middle Status of savagery, for example, the
> Australians and the greater part of the Polyne-
> sians when discovered. (1878, p. 10)

Yet when he approached the evolution of society by
moving backward through time, peeling away successive
institutions, Morgan placed the tribe in a relatively
late position within the "period of savagery" (1878,
p. 36). Although he was not averse to speculation,
Morgan may have judged it impossible to narrow down
the appearance of this great development, since no
living examples of pre-tribal organization could be
found. He did remain consistent in the order in which
he listed critical developments and shows the emergence of tribes as one of the last developments in the
period of lower savagery, leading to the succeeding
period with its first "unnatural" food supply (from
fishing). It was at this time that "mankind had
learned to support themselves in numbers. . . . In social organization, they had advanced from the consan-
guine horde into tribes organized in gentes, and thus
became possessed of the germs of the principal governmental institutions" (Morgan, 1878, pp. 526-527. Pace
Robert H. Lowie!).
    Morgan's view of property, in this context, is
very interesting:

> But the property of savages was inconsiderable.
> Their ideas concerning its value, its desire-
> ability and its inheritance were feeble. . . .

A passion for its possession had scarcely been
formed in their minds, because the thing itself
scarcely existed. It was left to the then distant period of civilization to develop into full
vitality that "greed of gain" (studium lucri),
which is now such a commanding force in the human
mind. Lands, as yet hardly a subject of property, were owned by the tribes in common, while
tenement houses were owned jointly by their occu-
pants. (Morgan, 1878, p. 528)

In Morgan's view, the succeeding status was lower barbarism, which saw the introduction of "a new species
of property, namely, cultivated lands or gardens. Although lands were owned in common by the tribe," group
or individual ownership appeared, but alienation was
not possible outside the limits of an effective kin
group (1878, p. 530). In the middle status of barbarism, said Morgan, there was an increase in personal
property "and some changes in the relations of persons
to land. The territorial domain still belonged to the
tribe in common; but a portion was not set apart" for
other uses such as government and religion. Kin
groups became more and more important as holders of
specific access rights, although patterns of inheritance were in some flux (Morgan, 1878, pp. 535, 537).
Further great transformations occurred in the upper
status of barbarism, to some extent recapitulating
previous developments, to some extent breaking new
ground and preparing the way for the emergent state
(and the status of civilization):

At the close of the Later Period of barbarism,
great changes had occurred in the tenure of
lands. . . . Lands among the Greeks were still
held . . . some by the tribes in common, some by
the phratry in common for religious uses, and
some by the gens in common; but the bulk of the
lands had fallen under individual ownership in
severalty. . . .

These several forms of ownership tend to show
that the oldest tenure, by which the land was
held, was by the tribe in common; that after its
cultivation began, a portion of the tribe lands

> was divided among the gentes. . . . ; and that this
> was followed, in the course of time, by allot-
> ments to individuals . . . (Morgan, 1878, p. 541)

Turning to Engels, let me simply assert that he accepted Morgan's main conclusion about the antiquity of
the tribe as a form of social organization, citing
only one example, a passage in which Engels remarks
that

> There can be no question that the tribes among
> whom inbreeding was restricted by this advance
> [to "Punaluan" family organization] were bound to
> develop more quickly and more fully than those
> among whom marriage between brothers and sisters
> remained the rule and the law. (Engels, 1972, p.
> 103)

As for ownership, Engels again takes a position
strongly based on the work of Morgan, for now the
concept of the gens has come to the fore, although the
tribe is still very much on the stage:

> . . . following Morgan, . . . we have the oppor-
> tunity of studying the organization of society
> which still has no state. . . . Among the North
> American Indians we see how an originally homoge-
> neous tribe gradually spreads over a huge conti-
> nent; how through division tribes become nations,
> entire groups of tribes; . . .

> But once the gens is given as the social unit we
> also see how the whole constitution of gentes,
> phratries, and tribes is almost necessarily
> bound to develop from this unit. . . . When we
> find a people with the gens as their social unit,
> we may therefore also look for an organization
> of the tribe similar to that here described . . .

> And a wonderful constitution it is, this gentile
> constitution. . . . All quarrels and disputes are
> settled by the whole of the community affected,
> by the gens or the tribe, or by the gentes among
> themselves; . . . Although there were many more
> matters to be settled in common than today—the
> household is maintained by a number of families
> in common and is communistic; the land belongs

> to the tribe, only the small gardens are allotted
> provisionally to the households. . . . (Engels,
> 1972a, pp. 158, 159)

The sequel was inevitable as the expansion of production, the growth of trade, the increasing development
of private property and concentration of wealth, among
other things, produced a social upheaval undermining
that "gentile constitution." Very important was the
growth of population, most particularly of the growing
heterogeneity of population replacing the previous
homogeneity of the tribe, in Engels' view.

> The gentile constitution was finished. It had
> been shattered by the division of labor and its
> result, the cleavage of society into classes.
> It was replaced by the state. (Engels, 1972a, p.
> 228)

Elsewhere, Engels says simply: "Tribes developed into
nations and states" (Engels, 1972b, p. 258).
    The formula is so simple and its acceptance, in
one guise or another, so widespread, that it must seem
a conceit to challenge it. Yet, in the latest English
edition of The Origin of the Family, Private Property
and the State, we find the following in a glossary
prepared by Eleanor Leacock:

> Tribe: The term generally used for groups who
> share a common language and culture, but who do
> not constitute historically evolved "nations."
> The term has been too loosely used, however. It
> has been applied alike to societies which are no
> more than a loose aggregate of autonomous vil-
> lages and to societies where there is a relative-
> ly centralized administrative and judicial appa-
> ratus. In many cases the development of formal
> tribal chieftainship has taken place as part of
> the struggle against colonial domination. The
> history of many North American Indian peoples
> exemplifies a transition from a more informal,
> to a "tribal," and then "national" organization
> and orientation. (Engels, 1972a, pp. 266-267)

This entire book is offered in support of Leacock's
charge of loose usage. Unfortunately, resort to

quotation marks does not provide amelioration: "tribe"
is really not much of an improvement on tribe.

   The use of the concept of tribe as a way station
in the evolution of the state violates ethnographic
knowledge. Theories that begin from false premises
cannot produce correct results. To remedy this situation, I suggest that we begin by jettisoning the term
tribe in most of its conventional uses. What is more,
with reference to this particular problem, we must attempt to think of the society of the time prior to the
emergence of the world's earliest pristine states as
it was in the absence of all states. When that condition prevailed, population densities and distributions
were very different from what was to follow. The relations among populations were also different. Not
necessarily entirely peaceful, I argue that they were
much less warlike. In any case, those pre-state societies were probably largely open; difficult to bound,
at their most structured, they were protean. Against
that background, I argue, the original, universal, and
very stable condition was egalitarian. This gave way,
under circumstances I have tried to indicate elsewhere
(Fried, 1967) to ranking: generally in communities.
This led, in turn, to stratification, and then to the
state. The pristine states originated as city states
or at least as fairly tight townships, not as precipi-
tates of closely defined tribes. The precipitation of
tribes, it seems to me, was triggered by the emergence
of the state, but did not really get into high gear
until the emergence of the ancient empires and, later
in a greater burst, after the appearance of colonialism and imperialism.

Chapter 12

The Tribe as a Secondary Phenomenon

I originally used the concept of secondary development with specific reference to the emergence of the
state, distinguishing those states that were "pristine" ("developed sui generis out of purely local conditions") from those that were "secondary" (societies
"pushed by one means or another toward a higher form
of organization by an external power which already
had been raised to statehood") (Fried, 1960, p. 729).
This usage was not invented by me, though I frankly
did not realize it at the time. A similar usage,
although not with regard to state formation, appears
in Marx:

> Communal production and communal ownership as
> found, e.g., in Peru, is evidently a secondary
> form introduced and transmitted by conquering
> tribes, who amongst themselves had been familiar
> with common ownership and communal production in
> the older and simpler form, such as occurs in
> India and among the Slavs. Similarly, the form
> found, e.g., among the Celts, in Wales appears
> to have been introduced there by more advanced
> conquerors, and thus to be secondary. (Marx,
> 1964, p. 88. Emphasis in original, cf. Marx,
> 1973, p. 490.)

It can be applied to many different situations, and I
think it appropriate, when the evidence is available,
to speak of "secondary ranking" and "secondary stratification" as well as "secondary tribes." In this

99

view, as I have indicated previously, tribalism can be seen as a reaction to the presence of one or more complex political structures, which is to say states, in its direct or indirect environment. Although Kroeber did not make this point in quite so general terms, we have already seen that he certainly discussed it with regard to the forms of organization found among Native American populations in the United States. (See the section on "The Notion of 'Tribelet.'" Another clear and specific example is available in Elizabeth Colson's study (1953) of the Makah Indians (cf. Fried, 1967, pp. 170-171), which describes the Makah as a tribe created by the Indian agency from an aggregation of formerly autonomous villages.

I have previously cited May Edel's analysis of the Chiga (Edel, 1965; Fried, 1967, pp. 171-173) as another clear case. Let me quote again a passage of hers since it provides an excellent introduction for more recent work in a similar vein.

> For such a people as the Chiga, whatever sense of ethnic unity they possess can only be an emergent one, a response to experiences of the recent past. For the Chiga as I knew them in the nineteen-thirties had no "tribal" unity whatsoever. . . . The only sense of common Chiga identity came from a common rejection of alien overlordship. (Edel, 1965, pp. 368-369)

Secondary tribal identity can result from hostile interaction, but other phenomena can also trigger it:

> Leach (1954, 1960) and Lehman (1963) have shown that a Southeast Asian society's membership in the set called "tribal" can be described, defined, and analyzed only in terms of that society's contrast to a civilized society which it may fight, serve, mimic, or even become—but which it can never ignore. Elsewhere (1965, p. 1216), I have argued that an individual is a member of some society by virtue of not being a member of other specific societies. In Southeast Asia, a society is a member of the tribal set by virtue of not being a member of the civilized set. (Moerman, 1968, p. 153)

The phenomenon of secondary tribal formation is
frequently so clear-cut that it is possible to date
its occurrence. As we have already seen, Elizabeth
Colson dated the formation of the Makah tribe from
about 1870. Other ethnographers have been just as explicit with regard to other secondary tribes: Aidan
Southall, talking about the Kavirondo of Kenya, a complex people that includes numerous named components,
identifies one of those components as the Luyia (Balu-
yia, Abaluyia) and adds that "the Luyia people came
into existence between approximately 1935 and 1945.
Before that time no such group existed either in its
own or anyone else's estimation" (Southall, 1970, p.
35).

There are many ways in which secondary tribes
can be precipitated; this essay is not the best place
to discuss them. Let me, however, make a few suggestions. First, the concept of "precipitation" is used
metaphorically, in its chemical sense, to suggest
emergence from latency. There is a reservoir of people and institutions that can be transformed by the
proper pressures (or "catalysts"); as implied, these
are several and diverse: there are many paths to secondary tribalism (and many to the secondary state).
There may be direct intervention by an existing state,
perhaps taking the form of a miniscule pristine state
beginning to enlarge itself, probing into its physical
surroundings. Some of the people it encounters may be
transformed into citizens, others into slaves, all
within the expanding system. Beyond, some of the peoples may resist and in the struggle find new organization as tribes: secondary tribes. Indeed, states with
somewhat greater sophistication may create tribes as a
means of ordering the areas immediately beyond the
territories being directly ruled. This is one of the
clearer dialectical processes: the gain in ease of exploitation and management of such secondary tribes is
differentially balanced by gains in military ef-
fectiveness by the new units. This process is visible
over a long period in the history of the Chinese
state. In their expansion toward the southwest, a
common technique used by the Chinese was the creation
of t'u-ssu ("tribal headmen"), persons raised to a
leadership that often had no prior manifestation among

the people concerned (cf. Fried, 1952; Wiens, 1954, pp. 201-266). The process was somewhat different and certainly more dramatic on China's northern and west-ern frontiers, where the outlines of the secondary formation were discerned years ago by Owen Lattimore:

> It does not seem likely that the feudal age in China was the result of the conquest of an agri-cultural people by mounted nomad warriors of the steppe. It is more probable that China contrib-uted to the creation of the steppe society by extruding fragments of "backward" groups. . . . (Lattimore, 1940, p. 408)

If secondary tribes can be precipitated by the direct intervention of superior organization, they can also arise as a consequence of economic penetration. Dealing with peoples beyond its borders, or marginals within them, a state may demand tribute, or demand levies so regularly as to comprise taxes. Whatever the imposts, the state may create or encourage new forms of organization to facilitate the siphoning off of the wealth of the less-developed societies. But secondary tribes can eventuate from nonofficial pres-sures or opportunities, such as the appearance of trade routes through the country, giving a chance for trade or plunder (if they can be differentiated). There are many different kinds of circumstances under which new (secondary) tribes can make their appear-ance. It is even possible, though I have no cases to cite, that tribes could appear as the result of ideo-logical pressures. Thus it is conceivable that mis-sionaries would forge such units to facilitate their task of conversion, or merely because they could not see the nonstate world except as comprised of tribes, so manufactured them to fulfill their own expecta-tions.

Did I say I have no cases of the ideological manufacture of secondary tribes? Actually, I think there are a great many of them. Particularly under modern conditions there is a premium placed on groups being able to bolster economic and political positions with claims derived from history. One Igbo (Ibo) an-thropologist remarks ruefully that "some Western writ-ers on the colonial era treated the Igbo as 'a people

without history.' We have since come to know better"
(Uchendu, 1965, p. 2). But Igbo history does present
a problem because Igbo identity comprises many smaller
ones. The Igbo "have no common tradition of origin.
It is only rather recently that some Igbo-speaking
communities have ceased to claim that they are not
Igbo" (Uchendu, 1965; see also Uchendu, 1970, pp. 56-
57; cf. Lloyd, 1969, p. 27). Another anthropologist
has attempted to place the Igbo and the tragedy of the
Biafran War in perspective:

> what we confront in Biafra is the consolidation
> of a modern people. Ironically, the war itself
> may set a similar process in motion in the more
> parochial areas of the federation. In any event,
> the basic dynamics of the Nigerian situation have
> never been predominantly tribal. The Hausa-
> Fulani-Yoruba-Ibo process of political conflict
> and accommodation before, during, and following
> formal independence is a function of the class,
> national, and neo colonial nature of the strug-
> gle in Nigeria, of the African struggle at large.
> Recourse to the explanatory principle of "tribal-
> ism" is a Western reification which blocks our
> view of African reality, and deflects our atten-
> tion from our own responsibility. (Diamond,
> 1970, pp. 26-27)

It is too early to be sure, but current news from Nigeria favors Diamond's analysis.

Secondary tribalism is a political phenomenon
bearing little resemblance to conventional notions of
tribal behavior. It occurs, as already indicated,
largely as a reaction to the presence of one or more
states. It is often goal-directed, although the ends
of the group are several, at various levels of consciousness and explication. Sometimes ends are confused or contradictory because secondary tribes are
usually stratified, with different classes seeking
different goals. Secondary tribes are heterogeneous
in other ways as well, some being extensively composite, comprising elements of population that previously were separated by considerable physical distances
and great cultural distances as well. This phenomenon
occurs within the boundaries of the United States and

may be one reason for the lack of unity in parts of
the American Indian political movement. Obviously, it
is something that may be exacerbated, consciously or
not, by the metropolitan power, in its own interest.

Secondary tribalism takes different forms and appears in various guises in the political processes of
states new and old. It may parallel the development
of political parties or manifest itself in bloc politics. It is obviously related to the phenomenon of
ethnic group formation, sometimes substituting for
it, at other times forming a portion of a larger process. It is much too large a phenomenon to be ade-
quately analyzed here. Let me conclude the subject,
then, with a simple warning: secondary tribalism cannot be analyzed in terms of vague conventional notions
about "tribes" and "tribalism," but must be approached
through our knowledge of stratification and the state,
colonialism, neocolonialism, and imperialism. The
concept of secondary tribalism enables us to resolve
some seeming paradoxes in recent political development, such as the apparent drag on the development of
modern politics in Africa, the continuation of ethnic
hostility and actual warfare within modern states in
Europe and elsewhere, and the apparently rising tide
of separatism, within the context of single unitary
states, of diverse "ethnic groups."

When a distinguished anthropologist says that the
"African is always tribalized, both in towns and in
rural areas" (Max Gluckman, cited in Cohen and Middleton, 1970, p. 3), one may wonder what he is thinking,
particularly if he has previously remarked that "the
moment an African crosses his tribal boundary to go to
the town, he is 'detribalized', out of the political
control of the tribe" (Gluckman, 1961, p. 69). Actually, Gluckman sees two kinds of tribal situation: in
rural areas the tribesman "lives and is controlled in
every activity in an organized system of tribal relations," while "in the urban areas tribal attachments
work within a setting of urban association" (Gluckman,
cited in Cohen and Middleton, 1970, p. 3). But neither of these alternatives provides any entry into what
I consider the realities of pre-state and state political organization. In the pre-state situation, to the
extent that any individual lives and is controlled in

an organized system of relations, that system is not
tribal but either communal (in the sense of pertaining
to a specific local group such as a village), or kinship group-oriented, or a combination of these two.
In the state situation, completely new principles come
into operation, as I have attempted to indicate.   Although it may be arrogant to state this, I must say
that at times Gluckman shows a glimmering of this
thought, as when he comments that

> this situation is not confined to Africans.
> Tribalism acts, though not as strongly, in Brit-
> ish towns: for in these Scots and Welsh and
> Irish, French, Jews, Lebanese, Africans, have
> their own associations, and their domestic life
> is ruled by their own national customs, insofar
> as British law and conditions allow.   But all
> may unite in political parties and in trade
> unions or employers federations.   Tribalism in
> the Central African towns is, in sharper form,
> the tribalism of all towns.   (Gluckman, 1965,
> p. 292)

Unfortunately, this discussion of secondary tribalism cannot be extended here.   Let me turn, then to
another topic which has often been confused: the relationship between tribe and nation.

Chapter 13

Tribe and Nation

The topic of "nation," including all its modern
complexities, is much more vast than the topic of
"tribe," so I intend in this brief section to touch
on only a few problems of high relevance to our main
concern with the tribe. Doing so, I must forego discussion of such important categories as "nation-
states," "nationalities," and the "nationality question," all of which provide some of the most fascinating problems for contemporary anthropological
analysis.[12]
     The etymology of the word "nation" helps us to
understand why it stands so close in meaning to
"tribe." Deriving from the Latin natus (past parti-
ciple of nasci, "to be born"), it suggests common
origin, a major connotation of "tribe." Indeed, a
current dictionary (Webster's Seventh New Collegiate)
conveniently indicates as part of its definition of
nation: "3: a tribe or federation of tribes (as of
American Indians)." A circle of meaning forms when
we encounter specific English-speaking American Indians using the word "nation" to cover a range of
organizational forms: thus in Angoon village, among
the Yakutat Tlingit, "people recognize that they form
a local community, but express this by saying that
they are a group of 'tribes,' or 'nations,' that is,
a group of sibs" (de Laguna, 1960, p. 26, cited in
Averkieva, 1971, p. 327). The confusion of types
also plagues professional social scientists, including
anthropologists. Perhaps one reason for this has been

106

advanced, albeit in another context, by Francis L. K.
Hsu who notes that: "It is probably true that the
'communities' actually studied by all anthropologists
in all tribes are about the same size, say, roughly
600 people or less" (Hsu, 1969, p. 6).[13]

A. L. Kroeber was concerned with the distinction
between nation and state; to a lesser extent he both-
ered about the difference between nation and nationality, but he recognized that the discussion took
place in very difficult semantic terrain:

> Politically, state and nation are one; as when we
> speak of the United Nations. But an essentially
> single nationality can comprise several states
> that in modern political terminology are called
> nations. . . . On the contrary, most large
> states, and especially empires, have comprised a
> variety of nationalities. (Kroeber, 1948, pp.
> 226-227)

Kroeber noted that part of the problem lay in the fact
that in conventional usage the word nation had two
contrasting meanings:

> First, nation denotes a people organized under
> one government, a "body politic." Second, a
> nation is a people of common origin, tradition,
> and language. (1948, p. 227)

With the mildest suggestion of irritation, Kroeber indicated what he believed to be a reasonable solution:

> Now the latter is just what a nationality is, by
> universal consent; and it would be fine if every-
> one would always use the word "nationality" when
> that was the meaning, and if "nation" on the con-
> trary were restricted to denoting politically
> organized peoples. (1948, p. 227)

Kroeber's favorite example for illuminating this distinction was the German nationality and state, but he
found the same condition to apply to Italy and France
and, indeed, "all over Europe" (Kroeber, 1963, p.
101).

Another anthropologist of Kroeber's generation,
John R. Swanton, was wary of dicta proclaiming the
meaning of either tribe or nation. Of tribe he remarked:

> As to tribes, even a superficial study of them,
> whether in America or elsewhere, will quickly
> dispel the idea that they are simple or perma-
> nent units, and one soon discovers that they
> present the most bewildering combinations and
> contradictions.
>
> In short, there is no one universally valid
> principle identifying a body of people as a
> tribe, and tribes or tribal groups varied so
> enormously as to dispose effectually of the idea
> that there was an immutability about them either
> in their origin or later development. (Swanton,
> 1942, pp. 1, 3)

About nation he felt much the same:

> On turning to examine the more advanced states or
> "nations" we find again a total lack of any one
> unifying principle or set of principles that
> would lend color to the dogma of an immutability
> in their number or their constitution. (1942,
> p. 4)

While neither Kroeber nor Swanton addressed himself to the problem of differentiating nation or nationality from tribe, others have tried to do so. One
of the main bases underlying such attempts is scale.
Tribal societies are viewed as pertaining essentially
to societies of small population; nations are relatively large. I. M. Lewis appears to support this
kind of distinction when he writes:

> a satisfactory characterization of tribal society
> must therefore concentrate upon criteria of form
> rather than of content. Here the most useful
> general criterion is that of "scale" (Wilson and
> Wilson, 1945). Ideally, tribal societies are
> small in scale, are restricted in the spatial and
> temporal range of their social, legal, and polit-
> ical relations, and possess a morality, religion,
> and world view of corresponding dimensions. . . .
> (Lewis, 1968, p. 147)

But Lewis is not altogether satisfied with this, for
he distinguishes "what might be described as a middle
range of large centralized states," in which he places

Baganda, Ruanda, Nupe, Zulu and the Iroquois Confederacy (1968). Admitting that in some respects "these examples do not conform fully to the ideal conception of a tribal society," Lewis concludes that:

> It is clear that the issue is not merely one of the degree of political and administrative centralization achieved, for there are many other tribal societies that lack these features and yet in terms of sheer numerical size assume the proportions of small nations. (1968, p. 147)

The examples cited include Galla, Somali, Yoruba, Hausa, and Ibo. Inclusion of the last three reminds us of another anthropologist's comment:

> the word "tribe" as applied to many West African societies lacks a precise meaning. When large population groups like the Igbo, Yoruba, and Hausa, each numbering over five million, possessing a common language, a similar "sense of historical experience," a common World View, and sharing a very strong sense of common identity in relation to other population groups—characteristics associated with national entities—are not terminologically distinguished from smaller descent groups, one wonders how absurd "convenient labels" can become. (Uchendu, 1970, p. 56)

But as we can see, the word "nation" is at least equally imprecise, a characteristic of the concept that has long attracted attention. Almost a century ago, at the Sorbonne, Ernest Renan was lecturing on the topic, "What is a Nation?" (Sait, 1938, p. 348; cf. Renan, 1939). Sait, a political scientist, pointed out that the range of opinions included many that were diametrically opposed. Thus, Ernest Barker is cited to the effect "that common language is not an essential characteristic, because the Swiss, with three or four languages, form a nation" (Sait, 1938, pp. 42-43, citing Barker, 1927, p. 13), while Carlton Hayes pronounced the Swiss not to be a nation, because they speak three or four languages (Sait, 1938, p. 43, citing Hayes, 1926, p. 8).

John Stuart Mill was one of many who saw a close relationship between nation and state, but that view

tends to be a normative one, rather than a simple observation of practice (Mill, 1931, p. 362). The disparity between peoples asserting nationality, on one
hand, and de facto states, on the other, is a commonplace. "Rarely, if ever, has the State coincided with
a previous identity of blood and language," wrote José
Ortega y Gasset (1932, p. 180). Indeed, Ortega went
on to assert that it was the state that precipitated
the nation. As Ernest Barker stated: "Historically
the State precedes the nation. It is not nations
which make States; it is States which make nations"
(Barker, 1927, p. 15).

If Ortega and Barker are right, and the main thesis of the present paper is valid, then the state
created the tribe and the nation and the self-
conscious nationality. I suspect that this suggestion
will find a cold welcome, as apparently these specific
ideas of Ortega and Barker have languished since their
appearance. Yet the two notions supplement and
strengthen each other. Nations are usually assumed to
have anticipated and provided the basis for state
formation precisely because it is imagined that pre-
state political development reached a zenith in the
emergence of populous tribes ruled by powerful chief-
tains.

Conversely, the notion of nation is rooted in
false and dangerous ideas of race. Homogeneity of descent is claimed and, whatever the genetic facts may
be, sanctified by myths that offer a common vision
held superior to reality. I cannot improve on Marvin
Harris's description:

> the European nations were complex heterogeneous
> supersocieties in which control over the state
> apparatus lingered on the outcome of domestic
> struggles no less fierce than those waged abroad.
> . . .
>
> It would seem undeniable that the wedding between
> racism and the doctrine of struggle was in part
> an excresence of this class and national warfare.
> . . . The fiction of common descent enshrined in
> the metaphor of fatherland and motherland, and
> applied indiscriminately to the overwhelmingly
> hybrid populations of Europe, improved the tone

of civil and military organization. The racial
interpretation of nationhood imparted to the
physical, cultural, and linguistic hodgepodges
known as England, France, Germany, etc., a sense
of community based on the illusion of a common
origin and the mirage of a common destiny.
(Harris, 1968, p. 106)

This, of course, is the phenomenon of bourgeois nationalism that is being portrayed, but the struggles
of the pre-capitalist state consumed its share of victims, fired up by their own diverse equivalents of
national myths. Saddest of all is the realization,
thrust upon us in the present century, that these   .
myths do not pertain merely to the bourgeois state or
its state-organized predecessors. The so-called so-
cialist states show an equally full panoply of nation-
alistic nonsense, beginning with the mandatory decla-
rations of fealty to motherland or fatherland, and
proceeding through the gamut of the violent reality of
war, not merely against capitalist rivals but social-
ist ones as well.

All too often the past is reconstructed as a projection of the fears of the present. Sometimes those
fears are magically exorcised by creating an image of
that past as a golden age; the fall from grace, at
least, gives some logical reason for the ensuing
troubles. At other times, and particularly in modern
academic disciplines, what frequently happens is that
specific nasty institutions, or their analogues, are
pushed deep into the past and thereby made virtually
synonymous with human nature, or at least with the
human condition. Thus the spectre of a fierce tribal
state underpins our conception of nations as ravaging
social entities. Ironically, the tribe, the rapa-
cious, violent tribe, may well be a product of the
state, or the state's philosophers.

Chapter 14

The Notion of Tribe

At the time this book was being written, the concept
of tribe was being frequently (as usual) evoked in the
media. A rock group called itself "The Tribe" and had
a record called Ethnic Stew, which included such songs
as "Think People" and "The World Should Learn to Party
Together." A book advertisement called attention to
"a spiritual journey which begins in the author's
'tribal village' of Malvern, Pennsylvania." A news-
paper quoted a Federal District judge saying that,
"The blunt fact is that an Indian tribe is sovereign
to the extent that the United States permits it to be
sovereign—neither more nor less." At stake was a
Blackfoot desire to operate slot machine gambling on
the reservation; it was not allowed (New York Times,
14 October, 1973, p. 32). At about the same time, the
House of Representatives approved HR 10717, a bill
that would repeal the act terminating Federal Government supervision over the members of the Menominee
tribe and their property. To clarify: it was in 1954
that Congress voted to stop dealing with the Menominee
as a separate body, agreeing instead to treat them as
individuals, with the goal of total assimilation. Now
we are in the process of a total reversal; the act
calls for the reinstatement of "all rights and privileges of the tribe or its members." Apparently un-
aware of the comment of the judge referred to above,
Representative Haley of Florida, called for passage of
the bill, asking Congress "to restore to the Menominee
Tribe of Wisconsin those Federal services furnished to

American Indians because of their status as American
Indians." This would make them once again "a federal-
ly recognized sovereign Indian tribe" (Congressional
Record, October 16, 1973: H9096-H9105; cited material
at H9096).

Examples of this kind can be multiplied almost
indefinitely. Indeed, some social scientists argue
that tribes and tribalism must be preserved for the
good of humanity. Jack Forbes (1969), for example,
argues that the social milieu of tribes and folk societies is much more conducive to mental health than
the pressure-ridden worlds of macroculture and macro-
society. He asks that tribes be preserved as an alternative mode of organization. Meanwhile another
anthropologist has suggested, albeit indirectly, that
professions are the "tribes" of contemporary life
(Boon, 1973, p. 2, citing Hymes, 1962). At the same
time, a cultural geography tells us that:

> The general availability in the United States
> of cheap domestic air travel and long-distance
> telephone communication may be effecting a
> "retribalizing" by renewing and strengthening
> intimate social compacts among members of fami-
> lies, communities, or ethnic groups otherwise
> widely dispersed by the complex spatial organi-
> zation of the economy. (Sopher, 1973, p. 116)

Another commentator has speculated that one of
the great benefits of the exploration of space will be
a rebirth of tribalism. The founding of small human
colonies throughout the galaxy will reconstitute small
tribal societies:

> Men's tribal instincts will move back from the
> destructive channels of nationalism, racism, and
> youthful alienation . . . genetic drift and di-
> versification will again become important factors
> in human progress. (Dyson, 1969, p. 13)

The combination of themes is interesting and raises
issues already touched on in this essay. The implica-
tion that tribal populations are closed has been shown
to be of dubious validity; the distinction between de-
structive nationalism and a more pacific tribalism,
however, is in my opinion a sound idea.

Early in this book I admitted that there was not much likelihood that I would be able to affect common or even professional usage of the word "tribe." This discussion has suggested that there is one usage that is in excellent accord with our knowledge and experience; this is tribe as a secondary sociopolitical phenomenon, brought about by the intercession of more complexly ordered societies, states in particular. I call this the "secondary tribe" and I believe that all the tribes with which we have experience are this kind. The "pristine tribe," on the other hand, is a creation of myth and legend, pertaining either to the golden ages of the noble savage or romantic barbarian, or to the twisted map of hell that is a projection of our own war-riven world.

If we have serious intentions of improving the world we live in, it is necessary that we deal with realities. Myths and legends are realities to the extent that they supply or subvert motives for social action. To act substantively on the content of a myth, however, is to be trapped by it. That is what happens when we succumb to an easy, conventional use of the concept of tribe. If you have read this far, you may still use the term tribe, but I expect it will be with a twinge of alarm and a new shock of recognition.

Notes

1. "The . . . <u>founder principle</u> emphasizes the fact that the smallness of the number of founders of a new group can give rise to a large drift effect. It should also be considered that a small number of founders implies that the number of individuals in the population must remain small for several successive generations, even though it will increase eventually. Thus, the total drift effect will be higher, the slower the reproduction of the founders." (Cavalli-Sforza and Bodmer, 1971, p. 417).

2. Waterman and Kroeber speak of 413 marriages but my addition of their tables yields the smaller total. See Waterman and Kroeber, 1934, p. 9.

3. But others say that the old Russian name "Samoyed" is derived from <u>same-edne</u> ("Land of the Saams"), and hence lacks derogatory meaning. See Dolgikh, 1962, p. 220.

4. This is a clear departure from the interpretations of both Malinowski and Uberoi. Although the latter does not accept Malinowski's assertions concerning the political authority and power of Trobriand chiefs, he does accept a much more stable situation than is seen by me. Thus, Uberoi does not question the assertion of absolute superiority of "Kiriwina District" and attributes it to three factors: intrinsic soil fertility; the existence of a district economy of largest scale; and extensive participation in the overseas

115

trading institution known as <u>kula</u> (Uberoi, 1971, pp. 43-44). In fact, little or no hard evidence is advanced to support any of these assertions. Malinowski himself was certainly inclined to make such statements, basing them on a synthesis of local beliefs and his own admittedly amateur impressions of soil types and conditions and quanta of agricultural productivity (see Malinowski, 1965, pp. 72-76, 459-460).

5. As in Kroeber's often cited remark: "Peasants . . . lack the isolation, the political autonomy, and the self-sufficiency of tribal populations. . . ." (Kroeber, 1948, p. 284).

6. Although this is not the place for criticism of general ethnological positions, I cannot refrain from noting what seems to be a static conception of band structure, revealed by this apposition of terms such as "sub-band" and "modern band." It seems to me that the rigidity of structure thus implied runs counter to the more and more widely accepted view that bands are protean, gaining and losing members, sometimes coalescing with similar groups, at other times pulling away, often with different cleavage points. Aware of these processes, Steward remarked that "'band' can have no precise definition" (Steward, 1970, p. 115).

7. In the period from 1884 to 1945, 146 such cases came before and were decided by the United States Court of Claims. Over 70 percent were dismissed without any awards. When awards were granted, they amounted to pittances—more than $2 billion was sought; awards came to about $38 million. See Stewart, 1961, pp. 181-182; cf. Barney, 1955.

8. The basic position stems from three distinct opinions handed down by the U.S. Supreme Court under John Marshall: <u>Johnson</u> v. <u>MacIntosh</u> (8 Wheaton 543, 1823), <u>Cherokee Nation</u> v. <u>Georgia</u> (5 Peters 1, 1831), and <u>Worcester</u> v. <u>Georgia</u> (6 Peters 515, 1832). (See Mc-Nickle, 1973, pp. 53-56). The position was reinforced in <u>United States</u> v. <u>Santa Fe Pacific Railroad Company</u> (314 U.S., p. 339), and the <u>Snake</u> case, U.S. Court of Claims (125 C. Cls., p. 241). (See Barney, 1955, pp. 320-321.)

9.   Some of the serious contexts in which this problem arises may be suggested by the following item from a commentary on recent events in South Africa: "Retribalization is designed to arrest the Africans' conception of a national consciousness and to encourage them to view their problems through the distorting prism of tribal particularism.   The division and dispersal of Africans along tribal lines isolate them from one another and from the Coloured and Indians." (Jordaan, 1973, p. 234.)

10.   There is an old word tribelet that refers to small cylindrical tubing, a mandrel-like tool employed by jewelers, but this word has no etymological relationship to the "tribelet" that interests us.

11.   Alas, it didn't last.   In 1971 Service brought out the second edition of his Primitive Social Organization and showed, with regard to the problem of tribe, that he really had not changed his position. This was confirmed in a recent, albeit more popularly written article (Service, 1973).

12.   This question is all the more fascinating for the author because of its reemergence as a problem in the People's Republic of China.   According to sources in the Soviet Union, the People's Republic of China has been having critical difficulties with minorities in the past several years (see The New York Times, 8 November, 1973, p. 3).

13.   Pace Robert F. Murphy (1971, p. 186), praxis displays critical weight—at least among anthropologists!

References Cited

Averkieva, Yu. P. (1961). "Problema sobstvennosti v sovremmenoi Amerikanskoi etnografi." Sovetskaya Etnografiya, 4: 200-213.

Averkieva, Julia (Yu. P.). (1971). "The Tlingit Indians." In E. B. Leacock and N. O. Lurie, eds., North American Indians in Historical Perspective, pp. 317-342. New York: Random House.

Barker, E. (1927). National Character and the Factors in its Formation. London: Methuen.

Barney, R. A. (1955). "Legal problems peculiar to Indian claims litigation." Ethnohistory, 2: 315-325.

Barnicot, N. A., D. P. Mukherjee, J. C. Woodburn, and F. J. Bennett (1972). "Dermatoglyphics of the Hadza of Tanzania." Human Biology, 44: 621-648.

Barrett, S. A. (1908). The Ethnogeography of the Pomo and Neighboring Indians. University of California Publications in American Archaeology and Ethnology, 6: 1-332.

Beals, R., and H. Hoijer (1959). An Introduction to Anthropology, 2nd ed. New York: Macmillan.

Berndt, R. M. (1962). Excess and Restraint: Social Control among a New Guinea Mountain People. Chicago: University of Chicago Press.

Berndt, R. M., and C. H. Berndt (1964). The World of the First Australians. Sydney: Ure Smith.

Bohannan, L. (1958). "Political aspects of Tiv social organization." In J. Middleton and D. Tait, eds., pp. 33-66. London: Routledge and Kegan Paul.

Bohanon, L. (1965). "Foreword." In B. B. Chapman,
    ed. Oklahoma City: Times-Journal Publishing Co.
Boon, J. A. (1973). "Further operations of 'culture'
    in anthropology: a synthesis of and for debate." In
    L. Schneider and C. Bonjean, eds., The Idea of Cul-
    ture in the Social Sciences, pp. 1-32. New York:
    Cambridge University Press.
Brokensha, D. (1966). Social Change at Larteh, Ghana.
    Oxford, Oxford University Press.
Brown, P. (1969). "Marriage in Chimbu." In Glasse
    and Meggitt, eds., pp. 77-95. Englewood Cliffs:
    Prentice-Hall.
Brown, P. (1951). "Patterns of authority in West
    Africa." Africa, 21: 261-278.
Buettner-Janusch, J. (1966). Origins of Man. New
    York: Wiley.
Buxton, J. (1958). "The Mandari of the Southern
    Sudan." In J. Middleton and D. Tait, eds., pp.
    67-96. London: Routledge and Kegan Paul.
California, State of. (1955). Progress Report to the
    Legislature by the Senate Interim Committee on Cali-
    fornia Indian Affairs. Sacramento: Senate of the
    State of California.
Cavalli-Sforza, L. L., and W. F. Bodmer (1971). The
    Genetics of Human Populations. San Francisco: Free-
    man.
Chagnon, N. A. (1968). "Yanomamö social organization
    and warfare." In M. Fried, M. Harris, and R.
    Murphy, eds., War: the Anthropology of Armed Con-
    flict and Aggression, pp. 109-159. Garden City:
    National History Press.
Chagnon, N. A., J. V. Neel, L. Weitkamp, H. Gersho-
    witz, and M. Ayers (1970). "The influence of cul-
    tural factors on the demography and pattern of gene
    flow from the Makiritare to the Yanomama Indians."
    American Journal of Physical Anthropology, 32:
    339-350.
Chapman, B. B. (1965). The Otoes and Missourias: A
    Study of Indian Removal and the Legal Aftermath.
    Okalhoma City: Times-Journal Publishing Co.
Cohen, R., and J. Middleton, eds., (1970). From Tribe
    to Nation in Africa. Studies in Incorporation Proc-
    esses. Scranton: Chandler.
Colson, E. (1953). The Makah Indians. Minneapolis:
    University of Minnesota Press.

Craig, Ruth (1969). "Marriage among the Telefolmin."
In R. M. Glasse and M. J. Meggitt, eds., Pigs,
Pearlshells, and Women, pp. 176-197. Englewood
Cliffs: Prentice-Hall.

Dalton, G., ed. (1967). Tribal and Peasant Economies;
Readings in Economic Anthropology. Garden City:
Natural History Press.

de Laguna, F. (1960). The Story of a Tlingit Community: a problem in the relationship between archeological, ethnological, and historical methods.
Washington, Bureau of American Ethnology, Bulletin
172.

de Laguna, F. (1972). Under Mount Saint Elias: The
History and Culture of the Yakutat Tlingit. Smithsonian Contributions to Anthropology, Vol. 7.

Diamond, S. (1970). "Reflections on the African revolution: the point of the Biafran case." Journal
of Asian and African Studies, 5: 16-27.

Dolgikh, B. O. (1962). "On the origin of the Ngana-
sans—preliminary remarks." In H. N. Michael, ed.,
Studies in Siberian Ethnogenesis. Arctic Institute
of North America, Anthropology of the North, Trans-
lations from Russian Sources, No. 2, pp. 220-298.
Toronto: University of Toronto Press. (Orig. ed.,
1952)

Douglas, M. (1962). The Lele of Kasia. London: Oxford University Press.

Driver, H. E., and A. L. Kroeber (1932). "Quantita-
tive expression of cultural relationships." University of California Publications in American
Archaeology and Ethnology, 31: 211-256.

Drucker, P. (1951). The Northern and Central Nootkan
Tribes. Bureau of American Ethnology, Bulletin 144.
Washington, U. S. Government Printing Office.

Dyson, F. (1969). "Human consequences of the exploration of space." Bulletin of the Atomic Scientists
25 (September): 8-10, 12.

Edel, M. M. (1965). "African tribalism: some reflections on Uganda." Political Science Quarterly, 80:
357-372.

Ehrenberg, V. (1960). The Greek State. London: Basil
Blackwell & Mott.

Engels, F. (1972a). The Origin of the Family, Private
Property and the State, with an introduction and

notes by Eleanor Burke Leacock. New York: International. (Orig. ed., 1884)

Engels, F. (1972b). "The part played by labor in the
transition from ape to man." In F. Engels, 1972,
pp. 251-264. New York: International. (Orig. ed.,
1876)

Firth, R. W. (1951). Elements of Social Organization.
London: Watts.

Forbes, J. D. (1969). "Tribes and masses: the self-
development of folk societies." Journal of Human
Relations, 17: 516-525.

Forde, C. D. (1951). The Yoruba-Speaking Peoples of
South-Western Nigeria. London: International African Institute.

Fortes, M., and E. E. Evans-Pritchard, eds. (1940).
African Political Systems. London: Oxford University Press.

Fried, M. H. (1952). "Land tenure, geography and
ecology in the contact of cultures." American
Journal of Economics and Sociology, 11: 391-412.

Fried, M. H. (1957). "The classification of corporate
unilineal descent groups." Journal of the Royal
Anthropological Institute, 87: 1-29.

Fried, M. H. (1960). "On the evolution of social
stratification and the state." In Stanley Diamond,
ed., Culture in History: Essays in Honor of Paul
Radin, pp. 713-731. New York: Columbia.

Fried, M. H. (1961). "Warfare, military organization,
and the evolution of society." Anthropologica, 3:
134-147.

Fried, M. H. (1967). The Evolution of Political Society. New York: Random House.

Fry, H. K. (1934). "Kinship in Western Central Australia." Oceania, 4: 472-478.

Gajdusek, D. C., and M. Alpers (1972). "Genetic studies in relation to Kuru. I. Cultural, historical,
and demographic background." American Journal of
Human Genetics, 24: 6 (Part II): S1-S38.

Gershowitz, H. M. L., Z. Layrisse, J. V. Neel, C.
Brewer, N. Chagnon, and M. Ayres (1970). "Gene
frequencies and microdifferentiation among the
Makiritare Indians. I. Eleven blood group systems
and the ABH-Le secretor traits: a note on Rh gene
frequency determinations." American Journal of
Human Genetics, 22: 515-525.

Gershowitz, H. M. L., M. Layrisse, Z. Layrisse, J. V.

Neel, N. Chagnon, and M. Ayres (1972). "The genetic structure of a tribal population, the Yanomama Indians: II. Eleven blood group systems and the ABH-Le secretor traits." Annals of Human Genetics, 35: 261-269.

Glasse, R. M. (1969). "Marriage in South Fore." In R. M. Glasse and M. J. Meggitt, eds., 1969, pp. 16-37. Englewood Cliffs: Prentice-Hall.

Glasse, R. M., and M. J. Meggitt, eds. (1969). Pigs, Pearlshells, and Women. Englewood Cliffs: Prentice-Hall.

Gluckman, M. (1961). "Anthropological problems arising from the African industrial revolution." In A. W. Southall, ed., Social Change in Modern Africa, pp. 67-82. Oxford: Oxford University Press.

Gluckman, M. (1965). Politics, Law and Ritual in Tribal Society. Oxford: Basil Blackwell.

Godelier, M. (1970). Sur les sociétés précapitalistes. Textes choisis de Marx Engels Lenine. Paris: Éditions Sociales.

Goody, J. R. (1969). Comparative Studies in Kinship. Stanford: Stanford University Press.

Gould, R. A. (1969). Yiwara: Foragers of the Australian Desert. New York: Scribners.

Gumpliwicz, L. (1899). The Outlines of Sociology, translated by Frederick W. Moore. Philadelphia: American Academy of Political and Social Science. (Orig. ed., 1885)

Gwaltney, J. L. (1971). "Myth charter in the minority-majority context." NEWSTATEments, 1: 34-40.

Harner, M. A. (1972). The Jivaro: People of the Sacred Waterfalls. New York: Doubleday/Natural History Press.

Harris, M. (1968). The Rise of Anthropological Theory. New York: Thomas Y. Crowell.

Hayes, C. J. H. (1926). Essays on Nationalism. New York: Macmillan.

Heizer, R. F. (1966). Languages, Territories, and Names of California Indian Tribes. Berkeley: University of California Press.

Helm, J., ed. (1968). Essays on the Problem of Tribe. Proceedings of the 1967 Annual Spring Meeting of the American Ethnological Society. Seattle: University of Washington Press.

Hickerson, H. (1967). "Some implications of the theory of the particularity, or 'atomism,' of the Northern Algonkians." Current Anthropology, 8: 313-343.

Hodge, F. W. (1910). "Tribe." In F. W. Hodge, ed., Handbook of American Indians North of Mexico, Vol. 2, pp. 814-819. Smithsonian Institution, Bureau of American Ethnology, Bulletin 30.

Hoebel, E. (1958). Man in the Primitive World, 2nd. ed. New York: McGraw-Hill.

Howitt, A. W. (1904). The Native Tribes of South-east Australia. London: Macmillan.

Hsu, F. L. K. (1969). The Study of Literate Civilizations. New York: Holt, Rinehart & Winston.

Hymes, D. H. (1962). "On studying the history of anthropology." Kroeber Anthropological Society Papers, 26: 81-86.

Hymes, D. H. (1968). "Linguistic problems in defining the concept of 'tribe'." In J. Helm, ed., 1968, pp. 23-48. Seattle: University of Washington Press.

Johnson, S. (1921). History of the Yorubas. London: Routledge.

Jordaan, K. (1973). "South Africa's dilemma: industrial pressure on racism." The Nation, 217: 233-237.

Krader, L. (1968). Formation of the State. Englewood Cliffs: Prentice-Hall.

Kroeber, A. L. (1932). The Patwin and Their Neighbors. University of California Publications in American Archaeology and Ethnology, 29: 253-423.

Kroeber, A. L. (1948). Anthropology. New York: Harcourt-Brace.

Kroeber, A. L. (1955). "Nature of the land-holding group." Ethnohistory, 2: 303-314.

Kroeber, A. L. (1963). "The nature of land-holding groups in aboriginal California." Aboriginal California (Robert F. Heizer, compiler), Berkeley, University of California. (Published for the University of California Archaeological Research Facility.) Pp. 81-120.

Langness, L. L. (1969). "Marriage in Bena Bena." In R. M. Glasse and M. J. Meggitt, eds., 1969, pp. 38-55. Englewood Cliffs: Prentice-Hall.

Lattimore, O. (1940). Inner Asian Frontiers of China. London: Oxford University Press.

Leach, E. R. (1954). The Political Systems of Highland Burma: A Study of Kachin Social Structure. Cambridge: Harvard University Press.

Leach, E. R. (1960). "The frontiers of 'Burma'." Comparative Studies in Society and History, 3: 49-68.

Legge, J. (1893-1895). The Chinese Classics. Vol. I,
  Confucian Analects, the Great Learning, and the
  Doctrine of Mean. Oxford: Clarendon.
Legum, C. (1970). "Tribal survival in the modern
  African political system." Journal of Asian and
  African Studies, 5: 102-112.
Lehman, F. K. (1963). The Structure of Chin Society.
  A Tribal People of Burma Adapted to a Non-western
  Civilization. Illinois Studies in Anthropology,
  No. 3. Urbana: University of Illinois Press.
Lévi-Strauss, C. (1969). The Elementary Structures of
  Kinship, translated by Rodney Needham. London: Eyre
  and Spottiswoode. (Orig. ed., 1949)
Lewis, I. M. (1968). "Tribal society," International
  Encyclopedia of the Social Sciences, Vol. 16, pp.
  146-151. New York: Macmillan/Free Press.
Lienhardt, G. (1958). "The Western Dinka." In J.
  Middleton and D. Tait, eds., Tribes Without Rulers,
  pp. 97-135. London: Routledge & Kegan Paul.
Lloyd, P. C. (1969). Africa in Social Change.
  Harmondsworth: Penguin.
Lowie, R. H. (1935). The Crow Indians. New York:
  Rinehart.
MacGregor, G. (1935). "Origin myth." In A. K.
  Kroeber, ed., Walapai Ethnography, pp. 12-26. Amer-
  ican Anthropological Association Memoirs, No. 42.
Maine, H. S. (1888). Lectures on the Early History of
  Institutions. New York: Holt. (Orig. ed., 1875).
Malinowski, B. (1921). "The primitive economics of
  the Trobriand Islanders." Economic Journal, 31:
  1-16.
Malinowski, B. (1937). "Anthropology as the Basis of
  Social Sciences." In R. B. Cattel, J. Cohen, and R.
  Travers, eds., Human Affairs, pp. 199-252. London:
  Macmillan.
Malinowski, B. (1965). Coral Gardens and Their Magic,
  2 vols. Bloomington: Indiana University Press.
  (Orig. ed., 1935).
Marx, K. (1964). Pre-Capitalist Economic Formations,
  translated by Jack Cohen. New York: International.
  (Original, 1857-1858)
Marx, K. (1973). Grundrisse: Foundations of the
  Critique of Political Economy, translated by Martin
  Nicolaus. New York: Vintage. (Original, 1857-1858)

Marx, K., and F. Engels (1959). "Excerpts from The German Ideology," translated by R. Pascal. In L. S. Feuer, ed., Marx and Engels. Basic Writings on Politics and Philosophy, pp. 246-261. Garden City: Doubleday/Anchor.

Marx, K., and F. Engels (1970). "L'Idéologie Allemande (1ère partie)." In M. Godelier, Sur les Sociétés Précapitalistes: Textes Choisis de Marx, Engels, Lenine, pp. 145-162. Paris: Editions Sociales. (Orig. ed., 1845-1846)

Mauss, M. (1966). "Essai sur le don: Forme et raison de l'échange dans les sociétés archaiques." In M. Mauss, Sociologie et Anthropologie. Paris: Presses Universitaires de France. (Orig. ed., 1923-1924)

McLennan, J. F. (1865). Primitive Marriage. Edinburgh: Adam & Charles Black.

McNickle, D'Arcy (1973). Native American Tribalism, Indian Survivals and Renewals. New York: Oxford University Press.

Meggitt, M. (1962). Desert People, A Study of the Walbiri Aborigines of Central Australia. Sydney: Angus & Robertson.

Middleton, J., and D. Tait, eds. (1958). Tribes Without Rulers. London: Routledge & Kegan Paul.

Mill, J. S. (1931). Utilitarianism, Liberty, and Representative Government. New York: Dutton. (Orig. ed., 1861)

Moerman, M. (1965). "Who Are the Lue?" American Anthropologist, 67: 1215-1230.

Moerman, M. (1968). "Being Lue: uses and abuses of ethnic identification." In J. Helm, 1968, pp. 153-169. Seattle: University of Washington Press.

Moret, A., and G. Davy (1923). Des clans aux empires; l'organization sociale chez les primitifs et dans l'Orient ancien. Paris: La Renaissance du Livre.

Moret, A. and G. Davy (1926). From Tribe to Empire, translated by V. Gordon Childe. New York: Knopf. (Orig. ed., 1923)

Morgan, L. H. (1878). Ancient Society. New York: Holt. (Orig. ed., 1877)

Murphy, R. F. (1971). The Dialectics of Social Life. Alarms and Excursions in Anthropological Theory. New York: Basic Books.

Nadel, S. F. (1947). The Nuba. Oxford: Oxford University Press.

Naroll, R. (1964). "On ethnic unit classification."
Current Anthropology, 5: 283-291, 306-312.

Naroll, R. (1968). "Who the Lue Are." In J. Helm,
1968, pp. 72-79. Seattle: University of Washington
Press.

Nash, M. (1964). "The organization of economic life."
In Sol Tax, ed., Horizons of Anthropology, pp. 171-
180. Chicago: Aldine.

Neel, J. V. (1969). "Some changing constraints on the
human evolutionary process." Proceedings of the XII
International Congress of Genetics, Vol. 3: 389-403.

Neal, J. V. (1972). "The genetic structure of a trib-
bal population, the Yanomama Indians." Annals of
Human Genetics, 35: 255-259.

Nimuedajú, C. (1948). "The Cawahib, Parintintin, and
their neighbors." In J. H. Steward, ed., Handbook
of South American Indians, Vol. III, The Tropical
Forest Tribes, pp. 283-297. Washington, U.S. Government Printing Office.

Oppenheimer, F. (1926). The State. Its History and
Development Viewed Sociologically. New York: Van-
guard. (Orig. ed., 1908)

Ortega y Gasset, J. (1932). The Revolt of the Masses.
New York: Norton.

Pelham, H. F., and R. S. Conway (1911). "Rome: ancient history." Encyclopaedia Britannica, 11th edition, Vol. 23: 615-619.

Radcliffe-Brown, A. R. (1952). "The comparative method in social anthropology." Journal of the Royal
Anthropological Institute, 81: 15-22.

Rappaport, R. A. (1967). Pigs for the Ancestors:
Ritual in the Ecology of a New Guinea People. New
Haven: Yale University Press.

Rappaport, R. A. (1971). "Ritual, sanctity, and cy-
bernetics." American Anthropologist, 73: 59-76.

Read, K. E. (1954). "Cultures of the Central Highlands, New Guinea." Southwestern Journal of Anthropology, 10: 1-43.

Renan, E. (1939). "What is a nation?" In A. Zimmern,
ed., Modern Political Doctrines, pp. 186-205. Oxford: Oxford University Press. (Orig. ed., 1882)

Ribeiro, D. (1968). The Civilizational Process, translated by Betty J. Meggers. Washington: Smithsonian
Insitution Press.

Ruey Yih-fu. (1972). "Hsi-nan shao-shu min-tsu ch'ung shou p'ien-fang ming-ming k'ao-lueh [On the Origin of Tribal Names with Insect-Beast Signified Radicals of Southwestern Minority Groups]," in Ruey Yih-fu, Chung-kuo Min-tsu Chi-ch'i Wen-hua Lun Kao [China: The Nation and Some Aspects of its Culture], Vol. I. Taipei, Yee Wen Publishing Co.: 73-117.

Sahlins, M. D. (1968). Tribesmen. Englewood Cliffs: Prentice-Hall.

Sahlins, M. D. (1972). Stone Age Economics. Chicago: Aldine-Atherton.

Sait, E. McC. (1938). Political Institutions. A Preface. New York: Appleton-Century.

Scott, J. G. (1910). The Burman, His Life and Notions, by Shway Yoe (pseud.). London: Macmillan.

Seagle, W. (1941). The Quest for Law. New York: Knopf.

Seligman, C. G. (1910). The Melanesians of British New Guinea. Cambridge: Cambridge University Press.

Seligman, C. G., and B. Z. Seligman (1932). Pagan Tribes of the Nilotic Sudan. London: Routledge.

Service, E. R. (1968). "War and our contemporary ancestors." In M. H. Fried, M. Harris, and R. Murphy, eds., War: the Anthropology of Armed Conflict and Aggression, pp. 160-167. Garden City: National History Press.

Service, E. R. (1971). Primitive Social Organization: An Evolutionary Perspective, 2nd ed. New York: Random House.

Service, E. R. (1973). "The ghosts of our ancestors." In Primitive Worlds: People Lost in Time, pp. 9-16. Washington: National Geographic Society.

Sharp, L. (1958). "People without politics." In V. L. Ray, ed., Systems of Political Control and Bureaucracy, pp. 1-8. Proceedings of the 1957 Annual Meeting of the American Ethnological Society. Seattle: University of Washington Press.

Sopher, D. (1973). "Place and location: notes on the spatial patterning of culture." In L. Schneider and C. Bonjean, eds., The Idea of Culture in the Social Sciences, pp. 101-117. New York: Cambridge University Press.

Southall, A. (1970). "The illusion of tribe." Journal of Asian and African Studies, 5: 28-50.

Spencer, H. (1896). Principles of Sociology. New
  York: Appleton. (Orig. ed., 1876)
Stern, T. (1965). The Klamath Tribe. Seattle: Univer-
  sity of Washington Press. (Orig. ed., 1936)
Steward, J. H. (1955a). "The composite hunting band."
  In J. H. Steward, Theory of Culture Change, pp. 143-
  150. Urbana: University of Illinois Press.
Steward, J. H. (1955b). "Theory and application in a
  social science." Ethnohistory, 2: 292-302.
Steward, J. H. (1970). "The foundations of basin-
  plateau Shoshonean society." In E. H. Swanson, Jr.
  ed., Languages and Cultures of Western North America:
  Essays in Honor of Sven S. Liljeblad, pp. 113-151.
  Pocatello: Idaho State University Press.
Steward, J. H., and A. Metraux (1948). "Tribes of the
  Peruvian and Ecuadorian Montana." In J. H. Steward,
  ed., Handbook of South American Indians. Vol. 3,
  The Tropical Forest Tribes, pp. 535-656. Washington:
  U.S. Government Printing Office.
Stewart, O. C. (1961). "Kroeber and the Indian Claims
  Commission Cases." Kroeber Anthropological Society
  Papers, 25: 181-190.
Swanton, J. R. (1942). The Evolution of Nations.
  Smithsonian Institution War Background Studies Num-
  ber Two. Washington: Smithsonian Institution.
Swedlund, A. C. (1972). "Observations on the concept
  of neighbourhood knowledge and the distribution of
  marriage distances." Annals of Human Genetics, 35:
  327-330.
Turney-High, H. H. (1941). Ethnography of the Kutenai.
  Memoirs of the American Anthropological Association,
  Number 56.
Tzu Yuan. (1962). Tzu-yüan cheng-hsü pien ho-ting pen.
  Taipei: Commercial Press. (Orig. ed., 1915)
Uberoi, J. P. Singh (1971). Politics of the Kula Ring.
  An Analysis of the Findings of Bronislaw Malinowski.
  Manchester: Manchester University Press. (Orig. ed.,
  1962)
Uchendu, V. C. (1965). The Igbo of Southeast Nigeria.
  New York: Holt, Rinehart & Winston.
Uchendu, V. C. (1970). "The passing of tribal man: a
  West African experience." Journal of Asian and Afri-
  can Studies, 5: 51-65.

Waterman, T. T., and A. L. Kroeber (1934). "Yurok marriages." University of California Publications in American Archaeology and Ethnology, 35: 1-14.

Wheeler, G.C.W.C. (1910). The Tribe and Intertribal Relations in Australia. London: Murray.

White, N. G., and P. A. Parsons (1973). "Genetic and socio-cultural differentiation in the Aborigines of Arnhem Land, Australia." American Journal of Physical Anthropology, 38: 5-14.

Wiens, H. J. (1954). China's March Toward the Tropics. Hamden: Shoe String Press.

Wilson, G., and M. H. Wilson (1945). The Analysis of Social Change Based on Observations in Central Africa. Cambridge: Cambridge University Press.

Wissler, C. (1922). The American Indian, 2nd edition. New York: Oxford University Press.

Wissler, C. (1923). Man and Culture. New York: Thomas Y. Crowell.

Zolberg, A. R. (1973). "Tribalism through corrective lenses." Foreign Affairs, 51: 728-739.

SUBJECT INDEX

INDEX OF PERSONAL NAMES

INDEX OF ETHNOGRAPHIC NAMES